CHINUA ACHEBE

Books by Tijan M. Sallah

When Africa Was a Young Woman (poems, 1980)
Before the New Earth (short stories, 1988)
Kora Land (poems, 1989)
Dreams of Dusty Roads (poems, 1993)
New Poets of West Africa (poetry anthology, 1995)
Wolof: The Heritage Library of African Peoples (ethnography, 1996)
The New African Poetry: An Anthology (poetry, 1999)

CHINUA ACHEBE:
TEACHER OF LIGHT
A BIOGRAPHY

TIJAN M. SALLAH

AND

NGOZI OKONJO-IWEALA

Africa World Press, Inc.

P.O. Box 1892
Trenton, NJ 08607

P.O. Box 48
Asmara, ERITREA

Africa World Press, Inc.

P.O. Box 1892
Trenton, NJ 08607

P.O. Box 48
Asmara. ERITREA

Copyright © 2003 Tijan M. Sallah and Ngozi Okonjo-Iweala
First Printing 2003

Book design: 'Damola Ifaturoti
Cover design: Roger Dormann

Library of Congress Cataloging-in-Publication Data

Sallah, Tijan M., 1958-
Chinua Achebe, teacher of light : a biography / by Tijan M. Sallah and Ngozi Okonjo-Iweala.
p. cm.
Includes bibliographical references and index.
ISBN 1-59221-031-7 (hardcover) --ISBN 1-59221-032-5 (pbk.)
1. Achebe, Chinua. 2. Authors, Nigerian--20th century--Biography. 3. Nigeria--life--20th century. I. Okonjo-Iweala, Ngozi. II. Title.

PR9387.9.A3 Z873 2003
823'.914--dc21

                                        2002152037

TABLE OF CONTENTS

DEDICATION

For
Onyinye, Uzodinma, Okechukwu,
Uchechi, Selly and Abass

MAPS

MODERN NIGERIA

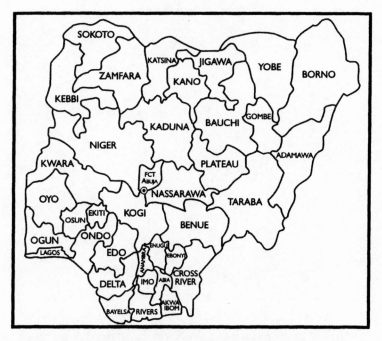

Map of modern Nigeria showing the 36 states and the Federal Capital Territory (FCT) Abuja

ACHEBE'S LANDSCAPE

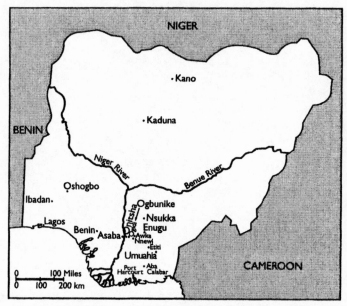

*Achebe's Landscape: map showing the cities and towns
of Chinua Achebe's home region in Eastern Nigeria*

ACKNOWLEDGMENTS

We are grateful to Chinua Achebe for allowing us to interview him in the early stages of this project, and for being responsive to our many subsequent queries as this project evolved. We have tried our best to clarify points of fact with him, so any error in this work is therefore ours.

We would like to thank Gary van Wyk and Professor Charles Larson for reading an earlier draft of the manuscript and for providing helpful comments, and Josephine Onwuemene for helping with the typing. Above all, we are most grateful to our families, especially to Ikemba Iweala and Fatim Haidara.

PREFACE

Though Chinua Achebe is arguably Africa's most famous novelist and one of this century's most important writers, few biographies of him have been published. This book, intended as a complementary text to Achebe's novels, aims to provide his life story to the general reader, especially to high school and college students. The specialist will also find much to admire in it.

Chinua Achebe has always played a vital role as a literary and moral leader, speaking out with a voice of reason and maintaining a strong vision for a revitalized Africa. He has been outspoken about hasty judgments and prejudice, and has urged instead that we open our minds to the deeper truths of Africa, the Africa not of crass television documentaries or snapshot journalism, but the Africa of lived truths that only the insider knows well.

During the 1967 Nigerian civil war (the Biafran war), Achebe, along with his family, relatives, and friends, suffered great hardships, but maintained his principled stance, vociferous in his objections to the injustices to Nigeria's Igbo peoples. In his writings, he has been equally forthright and visionary, ready to confront the shortcomings of Africa and Africans while simultaneously not letting Europeans, as is customary today, "off the hook," and critically examining their exploitative relationships with Nigeria, Africa, and black humanity in general.

We have chosen the title of this text, *Teacher of Light*, to contrast with Joseph Conrad's *Heart of Darkness*. Conrad's book did much to spread negative stereotypes about Africa: as a "dark continent," as the home of the "primitive" and the "savage." His book reveals the Europeans' enormous ignorance of the real Africa. Conrad's Africa was that of the ill-informed outsider, one whom Chinua Achebe has aptly described as seeing Africa through "a haze of distortions and cheap mystifications." In contrast, Chinua Achebe's Africa, as reflected in his writings, is full of restorative wisdom, conceived in the perspective of the informed insider, one who penetrates the surface, appreciates and reveals Africans as they are, unspoilt by the biased documentary and fictional account of the European's fabricated gaze. Achebe is able to use his accomplished powers of storytelling to *enlighten*, to *illuminate*, and, as he puts it, "to *teach*," helping African societies to "regain belief in themselves and put away the complexes of the years of denigration and self-abasement."

Preparing this book has led us to recall with nostalgia our own childhoods, respectively, in Gambia and Nigeria; in short, in West Africa. Despite Africa's current difficulties, we believe Chinua Achebe's life story will inspire and, above all, will especially challenge the youth of the world to dream and to act with confidence to achieve a brighter future.

Tijan M. Sallah and Ngozi Okonjo-Iweala
December 2002
Washington, D.C.

CHAPTER 1

Childhood in an Ogidi Family

Isaiah Okafor Achebe and Janet Anaenechi Iloegbunam Achebe looked at each other that day, and they were happy that a son had been born to them. The day was November 16, 1930. Several days later, the Achebes happily named their newborn Albert Chinualumogu Achebe. Though the anticipation had been long, the birth filled the parents and their relatives with joy, for among the Igbo a child is a very special gift.

In the Igbo language, *Chinualumogu*, shortened to *Chinua*, means "May *chi* (personal divinity or God) fight for me," and *Anichebe*, shortened to *Achebe*, means "May the earth goddess, Ani, protect." Chinua was baptized with the name Albert, as a tribute to the beloved husband of Great Britain's Queen Victoria. In later years, when Chinua Achebe went to university, he dropped "Albert," preferring to use his African name. Nevertheless, his mother insisted on using his English Christian name, and so did some of Chinua's early acquaintances.[1]

Chinua Achebe's birthplace is Ogidi, a town located in southeastern Nigeria. Today Ogidi is part of Anambra State, one of the Federal Republic of Nigeria's thirty-six states.

Chinua Achebe was born after the harvest season, when food, especially the main staple yam, was plentiful. As was the tradition, his family feasted on yams to celebrate his birth. In the Igboland of those days, yam was the king of all crops. Yam was considered a man's crop, because farming it required backbreaking toil, and the man who planted and harvested healthy yams truly earned the community's respect.

Chinua Achebe's father, Isaiah Okafor Achebe, came from the village of Ikenga in Ogidi. Isaiah's Igbo name, *Okafor*, was given to a son born on the Igbo market day of *Afor*. Although slight, Isaiah was so great a wrestler and spirit dancer that he was nicknamed "okra," suggesting that his body during a wrestling contest was as slippery as cooked okra. He was difficult to grab, and always quick to break out of a wrestling embrace, and easily threw his opponent to the ground.[2]

Named after the biblical prophet Isaiah, Okafor Achebe was first a school teacher. Then after his conversion to Christianity by the British missionary, Reverend S.R. Smith, who baptized him in 1902, he became a catechist for the Church Missionary Society (CMS),[3] an Anglican denomination. Both of Isaiah's parents died when he was young; so he never knew his parents. He was brought up by his maternal uncle, a great man who had garnered the second highest title bestowed to a man of wealth and honor in his village. The lavish feast he gave to celebrate his title earned him the name *Udo Osini*, "Udo who cooks more that the whole people can eat," as a tribute to his generosity.

Udo Osini did not object when Isaiah joined the Church of England. When Isaiah made efforts to convert Udo Osini, the old man said, "No, no, no," but nevertheless allowed Isaiah to follow his new faith. Udo Osini even allowed one of the earliest Christian missionaries in Igboland to operate from his compound, but later asked them to leave. "Your singing," Udo Osini told them, "is too sad to come from a man's house. My neighbors might think it was my funeral dirge."[4] The Anglicans left but decided to train Udo Osini's nephew for the ministry in the college, from which Isaiah had graduated in 1904 and had become an evangelist.

Isaiah Achebe began to teach and to spread the gospel, going from place to place, all over his district, and beyond, crossing Nigeria's largest river, the Niger, by canoe. Chinua Achebe did not realize how vast an area his father had covered until he himself traveled from Ogidi to Lagos. Given the poor roads in those days, he marveled that his father had covered most of this territory on foot.

In the year he retired in 1935, Isaiah Achebe returned with his family to his ancestral home of Ogidi with a pension of thirty shillings a month. He moved into his large house made of whitewashed earth walls and corrugated iron roof, a big improvement over the grass-roofed mission house he had then left.[5]

After his return, Isaiah Achebe preached a homecoming sermon in Ogidi at St. Phillip's Anglican Church, where he had been a co-founder. In the sermon, he reminisced about the early days of his missionary journeys in 1904, which to the nascent Christian congregation seemed a period so placed in antiquity that Isaiah was nicknamed "*Mister Nineteen-Four.*" Chinua Achebe recalled, "But worse was to come to my siblings and me at school as *Nineteen-Four's* children. I am not sure why I found the sobriquet as disagreeable as I did. In any event, it helped to fix in my mind the idea that Ogidi people were not very nice and that school was an unfriendly place."[6]

Chinua's mother, Janet Achebe, came from the village of Umuike in Awka, located about twenty miles away from Ogidi, and she was a descendant of blacksmiths. Family lore has it that Janet's father originated from a sacred cult of blacksmiths who lived in the general area of Umuahia before they moved to Awka. Chinua's parents met in Awka, an area renown for its blacksmiths, when Isaiah Achebe was in college. At the time, Isaiah Achebe was being trained at Awka's famous CMS college.

3

The blacksmiths of Awka plied their trade throughout Nigeria and returned home once a year for the major festival there. Wherever they traveled, they were valued and given shelter because of their unique skills. They would display a palm frond in front of their temporary homes as a sign of their trade, which indicated that an Awka person was living there.

For an Awka girl of that time, Janet Achebe had traveled extensively throughout all parts of Igboland. Her father had already died when she met Isaiah, her future husband; so Isaiah arranged for her education by the Anglican missionaries. She attended the well-known St. Monica's Girls' School in Iyi-enu, which the wives of the British missionaries founded in 1906. Iyi-enu was very close to Onitsha, a large market town about seven miles south of Ogidi. Janet Achebe received her education and lived with her teachers. She finally was married to Isaiah in 1909 at the Ebenezer Church in Ogidi. The couple was married by the celebrated British missionary turned anthropologist, Dr. G. T. Basden, who was Isaiah's teacher, supervisor, and friend. Basden was famous for his 1921 book, *Among the Ibos of Southern Nigeria*. As an inquisitive missionary-turned-amateur anthropologist, Basden became so involved and wrote so authoritatively about the Igbos that Ogidi honored him with a monument in the form of a carved ivory tusk.[7]

Chinua narrates his mother's struggles, noting that "as a special favor she went to live with the Principal, Edith Ashley Warner, and her small team of English teachers. She performed domestic chores in return for her education and upkeep. The daughter of a village blacksmith, she found her new life strange, exciting and sometimes frightening. Her most terrifying early experience was discovering one night in a bowl of water her mistress's dentures or, in my mother's words, her 'entire jaw.'" Chinua recalled pictures of Miss Warner hanging on their family wall in those days; he described her as being "quite good-looking and her jaw seemed all right in the photograph."[8]

Miss Warner once beat Chinua's mother because she had

laughed when the Victorian principal misused some Igbo verbs. "Later," Chinua noted, "she called her and gave her a lecture on good manners. 'If I speak your language badly, you should tell me the right way. It is wrong to laugh at me,' or words to that effect. My mother told that story many times...."[9]

Janet Achebe worked hard in the church, providing for her family and looking after the womenfolk while Isaiah Achebe evangelized. She grew cocoyams and vegetables, and supplemented her income with petty trading.

Chinua's mother and father were both literate, which was unusual in those times, and they instilled in their son the value of reading and enjoying books.

Chinua was fifth in a family of four boys and two girls, who all grew up well educated. His mother had given birth to other children, who had died because of the misfortune and poor medical care that ravaged families in those days. Chinua's oldest brother, Frank Okwuofu Achebe, worked in the Wireless Section of the Posts and Telegraphs Department until his retirement, when he returned, as the eldest son, to occupy his father's home. Frank died in 1992. John Chukwuemeka Ifeanyichukwu was the next eldest. Following his father's advice, John first worked as a teacher, then as a publisher, and finally became a pastor in the Anglican Church.[10]

Chinua's eldest sister, Zinobia Uzoma, was the third in line, followed by Augustine Nduka, then by Albert Chinualumogu, and lastly by Grace Nwanneka. Zinobia married a fellow teacher who later became a pastor. Augustine practised as a civil engineer. Grace taught for a while and then got married. Today both Zinobia and Grace are widows.[11]

At the time of Chinua Achebe's birth, his father was preaching at St. Simon's Church in Nnobi, a large town located about twelve miles southeast of Ogidi. Chinua grew up with Grace, his younger sister by three years, and the last child in the family. When Chinua Achebe began school, the family decided that Grace should begin too, to avoid being left home alone. In the absence of mom, big sister Zinobia Uzoma took care of them. At first Chinua was afraid of school and so fond of Zinobia that he would skip his classes and join Zinobia in her sixth grade class; however, the school soon put a stop to that.[12]

Zinobia, like her mother, was an entertaining storyteller. The young Chinua learned a great deal from her and grew up retaining many of her stories in his prodigious memory. As a child, Chinua never really got to know his brothers well because of the age difference between them. Before he began school, his older brothers were already working in faraway places such as Lagos, and the state of communications was very poor then. His family was like two families: one at home in the village; the other, the extended one, scattered throughout the towns and cities of Nigeria.

NOTES

1. Chinua Achebe, *Hopes and impediments* (New York: Bantam Doubleday, 1989), pp. 33-34.
2. Authors' interview with Chinua Achebe, March 1995.
3. Robert W. Wren, *Achebe's World* (Washington, D.C.: Three Continents Press, 1980), p.98.
4. Achebe, *Hopes and Impediments*, pp. 31-32.
5. Chinua Achebe, *Home and Exile* (Oxford: Oxford University Press, 2000), p. 2.
6. Ibid. p. 3.
7. Wren, *Achebe's World*, p. 18, pp. 98-100; Chinua Achebe, "The Education of a 'British Protected' Child," *The Cambridge Review*, 6(1993), p. 53.
8. Achebe, "Education of a 'British Protected' Child," p. 53.
9. Ibid., p. 53.
10. Gordon Lewis, "Interview with Chinua Achebe" in Bernth Lindfors (ed.) *Conversations with Chinua Achebe* (Jackson: University Press of Mississippi, 1997), p. 185.
11. Ibid., pp. 185-190.
12. Ibid.

CHAPTER 2

That Magical Place, Ogidi

C hinua Achebe's birthplace of Ogidi was a community of farmers, traders, masons, blacksmiths, woodcarvers, musicians, leather workers, and their shrines. There were also institutions representing the face of the British colonial empire, such as the post office, the Iyi-enu hospital, the two Anglican churches of St Phillips and Ebenezer, St. Vincent Roman Catholic church, and the American Faith Tabernacle church. The Ogidi community worked hard during the rainy season, but also played hard during festivals. Chinua Achebe described Ogidi as "just one of these hundreds of towns which were in reality ministates that cherished their individual identity but also, in a generic way, perceived themselves as Igbo people."[1] Ogidi's independence in running its daily practical life was a central feature of Igbo communities in general. As Chinua explained with the Igbo proverb, *nku di na mba na-egbelu mba nni,* "every community has enough firewood in its own forests for all the cooking it needs to do."[2]

Ogidi was a town of about five thousand people and one

thousand houses, and mostly unpaved streets. It was divided into nine sections, which could easily qualify independently as hamlets. Chinua's was called Ikenga. The main road divided Ogidi in half, and the Native Court was situated nearby. A chief or colonial district officer, who heard local cases and settled disputes, often presided over this court.

Although Ogidi was a town and its post office was small, the building was an important fixture. Located in the Native Court premises along the main road, the post office was a one-room building with a large front window that opened in the morning to serve as a counter. During Chinua's boyhood years, the local post master, fondly called P.M., was a tall young man who barely completed primary school, and the postman was another barely literate villager, who wore khaki uniforms and rode a bicycle to deliver mail.[3] These semi-literate servants of the empire were a source of local amusement, especially for the children.

Chinua noted, "I witnessed, as a child, the incorporation of my village into the vast network of postal services that knit the British Empire together, without, of course, understanding what I was seeing."[4] Institutions like the post office gave a real face to empire, but many Ogidi children, including Chinua's playmates, never fully understood their significance. For the children, the post office and its beehive activity broke the monotony of village life and added entertainment to the experiences of their young lives. Chinua recalled that Ogidi's "participation in a network of imperial transactions was made manifest in the daily coming and going at our post office. Other postmen came from surrounding towns and villages, bringing in letters in canvas bags secured with brass rings and locks, and taking away other bags. But the real event of the day was the majestic arrival of the six-wheeled, blue-painted lorry with the name Royal Mail emblazoned in big, yellow letters on its brow and on each flank."[5] The detailed description here suggests the attention and awe that these institutions of empire inspired among Chinua and his fellow playmates.

Around this time, of course, the automobile was a new invention. In further descriptions of the Royal Mail, Chinua recalled, "We, the children, had a special name for it, which we called out with the mixture of admiration and fear children can handle so well: *Ogbu-akwu-ugwo*, which means Killer-that-doesn't-pay-back, a rather strong name, you might say, for a truck that merely wanted to deliver the king's mail!"[6] While Chinua and his playmates did not fully understand this mean Igbo taunt, it was clear that the Royal Mail brought in and took away things. For the children, however, there was mystery in contemplating the nature of what it brought in and took away. "Although it was children I remember calling the Royal Mail by its terrible alias, I am pretty certain that the adults were responsible for creating it and letting it loose among us ostensibly for our education in road safety!"[7] In short, the village elders, uncertain about the consequences of the new colonial intrusion, wanted to keep their children cautious and safe.

As Ogidi opened itself to the bitter-sweet lure of the empire, it also held on to its rich Igbo traditions. Ogidi people were united around a totem, the royal python, which protected them from enemies. Sacred and secretive, the royal python was respected throughout the Idemili district in which Ogidi was situated. Ogidi was typical of the small, tight-knit communities in which Igbo peoples generally lived, unlike the vast kingdoms and empires in which some African peoples lived. Although a few Igbo kingdoms developed east of the river Niger, these were minor ones when compared with the large kingdoms of the Yoruba people of western Nigeria or of the Hausa people in northern Nigeria. Their fierce republicanism and preference for small living communities led some European observers to allege that the Igbos were too primitive to organize large communities. The Igbos, however, relate a different account in their stories. They speak of having

11

known those large communities but of not wanting them. Some stories even suggest that Igbos had large communities in the past but chose to abandon them because they became oppressive.[8]

Democratic village organization was, therefore, the social character of Igbo communities. Igbo communities valued the individual. Everyone in the general village assembly partipated in making social decisions. The titled men and women, who had risen through their own hard work in the village and had gradually developed their power and influence, provided leadership.

Two major social practices, both unattractive to Christian missionaries, characterized the Igbo and contradicts the Igbo's otherwise egalitarian social organization: one was the killing of twins, whose birth was considered a curse that would bring calamity. The Igbo believed human beings should have only one offspring during every birth. Having more in a single birth was considered a foul act of degrading human beings to the level of animals. As the Igbo people say, "Plural offspring is nature's law for goats, cats and dogs, not for men."[9] Another "unattractive" Igbo practice was the social contempt they held for the *Osu* or *cult slave*, people who were feared, hated and considered *unclean*. The *Osu* were often captured individuals, non-native to the community, given to a deity to carry the sins of their owner, and the system was hereditary.[10] They were in, short, sacrificial lambs.

Although Chinua knew these aspects of his people, he grew up probing the complexities of his culture and loving in particular each villager's open participation in Ogidi's affairs. Although there were distinctions of sex, age, and wealth, no individual exercised enormous control over the lives of others. Every villager had an opportunity to make something of his or her life. Chinua loved the Igbo proverb, "When a child washes his hands, he deserves to eat with his elders." When public matters were thrown open for discussion, they were done in the open square, where all of the roads of the village meet. After hearing every villager, men of respect and prestige considered the different views, reached a decision, and then asked the most outspoken person among them to announce the decision to the general assembly. The decision was then approved or rejected by the assembly. This exercise in direct democracy emphasized transparency, or bringing all public matters to be candidly discussed in the open, at its core.[11]

Farming was the main occupation in Chinua's native Ogidi, and root crops such as yam, cocoyam, and cassava dominated and were planted to provide for subsistence needs. Men grew mostly yams, but also tree crops such as oil palm, bananas, papaya, mangos, breadfruits, plantain, kola nuts, oranges, pears and *iroko*— the tallest tree in Igboland, which provided hardwood or timber for building purposes. Yam was a crop from which hardworking men obtained recognition through "yam titles." Women grew melons, maize, okra, beans, peppers, pumpkins, sometimes between the spaces of the yam crop. There was also a variety of wild vegetables such as mushrooms. Various foods and drinks were prepared, such as the staple *nniakpu* or "pounded cassava," and palmwine, the fermented juice of the oil palm tree stored in gourds.[12]

Competition among Igbo communities has been a constant throughout Igbo history. At its worst, it led to conflict. At its best, it brought out the energy and dynamism of the Igbo.[13] Typical of Igbo villages, the men and elderly women ran Ogidi's affairs according to their age, title and occupation, and some women handled domestic chores as well as ran the vibrant network of markets, including managing the four-day markets. The four market days were: *nkwo*, the busiest; followed by *eke*, *oye*, and *afor*. Boys were given names based on the market day they were born, as follows: Nwa*nkwo*, Nw*eke*, Nw*oye*, and Nw*afor*, or Oko*nkwo*, Ok*eke*, Ok*oye*, and Ok*afor*. Girls were similarly given names corresponding to the market day: Anda*nkwo*, Ad*eke*, Ad*oye*, and Ad*afor*, or Mgbo*nkwo*, Mgb*eke*,

Mgb*oye*, and Mgb*afor*. In markets, they traded ideas and goods such as yams, palm oil, cassava, okra, melons, mushrooms, and at the same time reinforced community solidarity.[14]

Community recreation involved wrestling contests between various neighborhoods and extended families of villages and towns, usually held against a background of engaging music and dancing. Many festivals united Ogidi and nearby villages and were designed to create harmony between communities and their oracles, spirits, and gods.

The most important and liveliest celebration in Ogidi was *Nwafor*, which was held in the middle of the rainy season, after completion of the back-breaking work of the planting. Nwafor was celebrated with feasting, kegs of palmwine, and several colorful masquerades. Among the most impressive were the *Bullroarer* (which appeared at night), *Agaba Idu* (a lion of the mythical land called *Idu*), *Akataka* (a scary being), and *Omanu Kwue* (if you know, speak), which was of "such towering height."[15] The night masquerades were often quite sensational. Many powerful masks appeared in the light of bonfires whose leaping flames illuminated the terrific beauty of the masks and costumes.

The variety of masks worn during Nwafor covered all human experience: "from youth to age; from playfulness to terror; from the delicate beauty of the maiden spirit, *agbogho mmuo*, to the candid ugliness of *njo ka-oya*, 'ugliness greater than disease'; from the athleticism of *ogolo* to the legless and armless inertia of *ebu-ebu*, a loquacious masquerade...." The masquerades involved sculpture, music, painting, drama, costumery, architecture, and movement. Chinua explained that to "enjoy [their] motion fully" the spectator "must follow [their] progress up and down the arena."[16] Watching masquerades later influenced Chinua's views on art and literature. He often cited the Igbo proverb to express his approach to art: "*Ada-akwu ofu ebe enene mmuo*, 'You do not stand in one place to watch a masquerade.'"[17] Life itself was a masquerade, and movement and observing it from different angles was central to appreciating its wholeness.

Chinua not only watched the Nwafor masquerades with the same delight as the other children, he closely observed the people, words, and events around him and stored his impressions in his extraordinary memory. The wise words of the Igbo elders, both at home and in the streets, and the tales they told about the Igbo stuck in Chinua's mind. Igbo life, customs, and outlook gave meaning to his own life and fired his imagination. Chinua recalled:

> My father's half-brother was not the only "heathen" in our extended family; if anything, he was among the majority. Our home was open to them all, and my father received his peers and relatives— Christian or not —with kola nut and palmwine in that piazza, just as my mother received her visitors in the parlor. It was from the conversations and disagreements in these rooms, especially the piazza, that I learned much of what I know and have come to value about my history and culture. Many a time what I heard in those days, just hanging around my father and his peers, only became clear to me years and even decades later.[18]

Chinua's experience of participating in and listening to conversations with villagers in Ogidi, their artistic use of words, prepared him for his mission as storyteller. He was to be a master griot or, to use Guinean writer Camara Laye's words, a "guardian of the word." As a linguistically gifted insider-storyteller, he told everything he saw and heard.

Notes

1. Achebe, *Home and Exile*, p. 6.
2. Ibid., p. 7.
3. Ibid., p. 76.
4. Ibid.
5. Ibid., pp. 76-77.
6. Ibid., p. 77.
7. Ibid., p. 78.
8. Authors' interview with Achebe, op. cit.
9. Victor C. Uchendu, *The Igbo of Southeast Nigeria* (New York: Harcourt Brace Jovanovich, 1965), p. 9.
10. Ibid., pp. 89-90.
11. Ibid., pp. 41-42.
12. Ibid., pp. 24-26.
13. Achebe, *Home and Exile*, p. 7.
14. Phone conversation with Achebe, September 2000.
15. Ezenwa-Ohaeto, *Chinua Achebe: A Biography* (Bloomington, Indiana University Press, 1997), p. 2.
16. Achebe, *Hopes and Impediments*, p. 66.
17. Ibid., p. 65.
18. Achebe, *Home and Exile*, pp. 10-11.

CHAPTER 3

At the Crossroads, Between Worlds

Chinua Achebe described the Ogidi of his early life as a "crossroads of cultures."[1] Although surrounded and strongly influenced by traditional Igbo culture, the influence of Britain, which ruled over colonial Nigeria, cut across Igbo tradition. Many Igbo believed that the aim of British colonialism was to penetrate the minds of the Igbo people and thus to alienate them from their own values. In their view, Christianity came hand in hand with colonialism to pacify the spirit and the resistance of the Igbo, so that colonialism could conquer their bodies.

Nevertheless Christianity and colonialism had only limited success in Igboland. Christianity, in particular, did not easily win converts. As Chinua noted, "Christianity did not sweep through Igboland like wild fire. One illustration will suffice. The first missionaries came to the Niger River town of Onitsha in 1857. From that beachhead they finally reached my town, Ogidi, in 1892. Now the distance from Onitsha to Ogidi is only seven miles. Seven miles in thirty-five years, that is, one mile every five years. A very slow walk by any standard!"[2] But

Christianity's slow walk did sweep up Chinua's parents and turn them into die-hard Christians.

For Chinua's mother and father, staunch but enlightened Christians, reason was central to their very existence and to their faith. In the zinc or corrugated-iron roof house that Chinua's father built in Ogidi, the front room according to missionary usage was called a piazza. Later Chinua would learn that their piazza had an unusual history. His father's younger half-brother, whom Isaiah Achebe had tried unsuccessfully to convert to Christianity, was asked to look after the zinc house before Isaiah retired. While caring for the house, Chinua's uncle comfortably converted the piazza into a shrine to the Igbo gods, placing his *ikenga, wooden idol,* and other divinities there, much to Isaiah's scandalized discovery. Chinua humorously described the frictions at this crossroad:

> My father was furious and demanded the immediate re-
> moval of the shrine not only from the house but from the
> compound. Perhaps that was the real cause of the coolness
> between them. I never did ask my father if he had the
> house reconsecrated after my uncle's brief tenancy and des-
> ecration.... Could he have been thinking of the irony of spend-
> ing his years converting strangers in far-flung parts of Olu
> and Igbo while Satan in the shape of his half-brother was
> hard at work . . . in the very front room of his own house at
> home?[3]

In Chinua's childhood home, however, Igbo beliefs still dominated, although half the village had converted to Christianity.
He recalled that, "on one arm of the cross, we sang hymns
and read the Bible night and day. On the other, my father's
brother and his family, blinded by 'heathenism,' offered food
to idols."[4] For Chinua, there was no tension or spiritual agony
existing between two cultures: "That was how it was supposed
to be anyhow."[5] Quite comfortable with the traditional ways
of his non-Christianized relatives and neighbors, he noted, "I

never found their rice and stew to have the flavor of idolatory."[6] Steeped early in Igbo pragmatism, Chinua absorbed both Christian and Igbo values.

Chinua's youthful ambivalence is reflected in his writing. As a young man, he enjoyed the parables and other moral narratives in the Bible, the admonition of prophets when things went awry, and the parallels in his native Igbo storytelling. He was puzzled by the superior attitude of his Christianized relatives, who referred to the non-Christian converts as "heathens" or "people of nothing." Chinua noted, "I have been absorbing the culture of my community from birth. I was brought up in a village. My parents were church people, Christians. The so-called people of nothing have quite a lot- the dancing, the masquerade, etc,- going for them. ...I never meant to say Christianity was wrong, but I believe there are some things worth the attention of others in the non-Christian sector."[7] Ever the mediator, preferring balance to extremes, he devoted his early life to openness to both Christianity and Igbo religion and values.

The traditional religion of the Igbo particularly values the concept of *chi, the "personal god force, spirit being."* The Igbo are a religious people, and their religious tenets include many major and minor deities who rule the living. The religion gives each person the ability to improve his or her situation either in the world of the living or, through reincarnation, in the world of the ancestors. The Igbos, who share a common language that is spoken in various dialects throughout eastern Nigeria, believe that *Chukwu Abiama* is the *"highest god."* He is the creator of the universe and its creatures, and he watches all creation from a distance, giving each person his or her own free will. The missionaries sought to Christianize the Igbo pantheon by equating *Chukwu* with *Jehovah* or *God.* In the Igbo pantheon, minor gods intercede with people and *Chukwu,* just as some Christians believe that saints intercede with people and God.[8] The Igbo also believe in *Agbara,* a type of devil, who is the cause of all evil. *Agbara* is seen as *Chukwu's* rival in the battle for Igbo souls.[9]

Subordinate to *Chukwu*, secondary deities rule different aspects of nature. These "nature gods" are not classified by rank or status; rather they are regarded as equals, much like the individuals in an Igbo village. The nature gods serve and protect their followers and help them advance towards their human goals. One of the most popular of the nature gods is *Ala*, also called *Ani*, the earth-goddess and great mother, the supporter of Igbo life who increases the fertility of the people and their land. Other minor gods include *Anyanwu*, the sun god who makes crops grow, and *Amadiora*, the lightning spirit who sparks energy and derives his power from the sun god. *Igwe*, the sky god, provides rainwater for drinking, washing, and farming.[10]

At an early age, Chinua steadily discovered that the Igbo do not have a rigid and closed theology to explain the place of human beings in the universe. Instead, they use poetry, myth, and other metaphors to describe the supernatural and to connect them with the spiritual world. Their religion is rich in folktales, proverbs, rituals, festivals, and songs. While these metaphors help to build an attitude of wonder, they also reinforce submission to the gods and respect for commonly held values.

During worship, the Igbo use wooden sculptures called *ikenga*. Today, these religious objects are regarded as works of art. Rather than objects of worship, like the Christian cross, these objects are signs that pave a way to the spiritual world. The *ikenga* bring the world of gods and spirits closer, thus enabling ordinary people to focus devoutly during worship.[11]

Among all the powers of the Igbo spiritual world, Chinua was most fascinated by the concept of *chi*. The Igbo believe that each person has a *chi* or "spirit being" who is a guide, protector, and guard. This *chi* determines each person's success or failure and time of death, and although the *chi* strongly influences a person's destiny, the Igbo believe that one can still exercise some choice and responsibility over one's existence. People with strength of character can influence their *chi* and direct their destiny positively. One Igbo saying adroitly expresses this belief: "When a man agrees, his *chi* also agrees." Many Igbo regard Chinua Achebe, himself, as an example of someone who has succeeded by positively influencing his *chi*.[12]

NOTES

1. Achebe, *Hopes and Impediments*, p. 34.
2. Achebe, "Education of a 'British Protected' Child," p. 52.
3. Achebe, *Home and Exile*, p. 10.
4. Achebe, *Hopes and Impediments*, p. 35.
5 Ibid.
6 Ibid.
7 Awogbemila et. al., "The Master Craftsman: Tribute to a Thinker and Writer at 59," *This Week*, 152 (1989), p. 16.
8. Uchendu, *The Igbo of Southeast Nigeria*, p. 95.
9. Ibid., p. 94.
10. Ibid., pp. 95-97.
11. Wren, *Achebe's World*, pp. 42-43.
12. Achebe, *Hopes and Impediments*, pp. 57-58.

CHAPTER 4

The Challenge of Empire

C hinua Achebe grew up in colonial Nigeria, which was created by the British in 1914. Cultural groups that had long existed as independent nation-states and had sometimes been hostile to one another were merged into one country under Lord Frederick Lugard, who would later devise the system of "indirect rule" to govern the colony. In mixing different groups under their administration, the British created a complex country composed of multiple languages and religions that functioned only through use of a single *lingua franca*: English.[1]

Today, Nigeria's population of 120 million is composed of 350 distinct language groups. The three largest are the Hausa-Fulani, found mainly in the north of the country; the Yoruba, in the southwest; and the Igbo, in the southeast. Other large groups include the Kanuri in the north, the Tiv in the middle belt, and the Ibibio, Edo, Ijaw, Itsekiri and Urhobo in the south. By merging many different ethnic groups into Nigeria, the British capitalized on historical suspicions among these groups to further their own interests through a colonial policy of "*divide and rule.*"

Islam, Christianity and traditional religions are all practiced in modern Nigeria. About fifty percent of the total population is moslem and concentrated mainly in the north of the country and in parts of the southwest. Arab traders and merchants from North Africa and Arabia brought Islam to northern Nigeria as early as 1000 A.D.. Much of the north had converted to Islam by 1600 A.D.. The remaining fifty percent of Nigerians are mainly Christian, concentrated in the middle belt and in the south. It is the British who introduced Christianity to the region. Although these major world religions have taken hold, many still mix them with traditional religious practices. A small percentage of the population remain strict practitioners of the indigenous religions.

Beginning in the 1800s, British colonialism in Nigeria was part of the larger scheme of European empire building. During this period, many European powers, especially Britain and France, struggled to acquire overseas colonies and to impose their authority over rival spheres of influence. At the Berlin Africa Conference of 1884, the European powers partitioned Africa for profit. Because of its pioneering history in science and its superior naval forces, Great Britain acquired the largest number of colonies. The British, particularly during the Victorian period, regarded themselves as leaders of a civilization whose main responsibility was to spread industry and progress globally. The private enterprise that was so successfully unleashed at home by "free minds, free markets, and Christian morality" was to be spread all over the world.[2] The British regarded it their duty to spread their own image of a multicultural nation- consisting of English, Scots, Welsh, and Irish united by the English language- as the universal ideal. The Irish were the first victims of this empire, since they increasingly lost their ethnic tongue to English, but were also somewhat its beneficiaries. The British established colonies in

North America, the Caribbean, Sub-saharan Africa, the Indian subcontinent, Australia, parts of South East Asia and the Pacific, and for some time parts of the Middle East.[3] They spread their institutions, culture, and language and transformed the peoples they colonized and also were, to some extent, transformed by them.

In Nigeria's Igboland, the effects of British colonialism were particularly dramatic. The British needed an ideology and a system in order to succeed. The colonial officials ignored Igbo history and regarded themselves as superior. Three factors worked in their favor. They had the maxim gun, which gave them power and military advantage. They had imperial support; their empire had spread and dominated the world, which gave them global advantage. They had the pen; the power of documentation gave them advantage over a society based on oral tradition and enabled them to glorify their image in the context of Igbo history to further their interests. With these advantages over the Igbo, especially with the absence of written records in Igboland, the British mistakenly believed that the history of these indigenous people began with their arrival. Igbo culture was denigrated, and Igbo beliefs were defiled as pagan "superstition" or "heathenism." Although the British found well-organized indigenous societies and vibrant oral traditions, they concentrated their efforts on turning the Igbo into part of their global empire.

At the beginning of the 1900s, the British imposed the system of *"direct rule"* over the Igbos. Igbo territory was carved up into districts, each ruled by a British district commissioner. A few Igbo were apppointed as clerks and messengers to help administer British rule. The British mostly promoted Igbo with low social status and little commitment to their own people. These Igbo workers and administrators, uplifted by working for their imperial masters, served with vigor and loyalty. Most Igbo, however, hated the whole system because it undermined their own democratic society.[4]

In 1914, Lord Lugard introduced a different system of colonial rule throughout Nigeria known as *"indirect rule"*; that is, a system of ruling Africans through their own traditional rulers. It was established first in the Protectorate of Northern Nigeria (among the Hausa/Fulani peoples) and then extended to the Protectorate of Southern Nigeria (among the Igbos, Yorubas, Edos, and other Nigerian groups). Under indirect rule, the old system of district commissioners was replaced with "traditional rulers" or "warrant chiefs." Given the democratic organization of Igbo society, indirect rule did not work well. Abuses were rampant, which resulted in a change in the system to comply more with traditional Igbo groupings and institutions. The new system survived until Nigeria's independence in 1960.[5]

For Chinua Achebe, colonial rule in Igboland was simply wrong. He forthrightly expressed his opposition to colonialism: "I will simply state my fundamental objection to colonial rule. In my view it is a gross crime for anyone to impose himself on another, seize his land and his history and then compound this by making out that the victim is some kind of ward or minor requiring protection. Even the aggressor knows this, which is why he will sometimes camouflage his brigandage with such brazen hypocrisy."[6]

Chinua Achebe regarded colonialism in Africa as one giant European project to rob Africans of their minds, to follow that with the robbery of their resources, and then finally to blame Africans for their incompetence. Consequently, he saw his task as a writer to reconstruct the African mind, to restore a narrative that has been unbalanced by the power of Europe and its storytellers. He has therefore challenged many icons of European civilization, such as Albert Schweitzer and Joseph Conrad, regarding their biased views of Africa.

In European attitudes and writings, Chinua saw a level of comfort linked to their strong will to dominate the world. He was surprised by Schweitzer's own failure to "see the most obvious fact about Africa"; i.e., that Africans were people, and also that no one had taken Schweitzer to task for his "blasphemy" in declaring: "The African is indeed my brother, but my junior brother." Similarly, Chinua was surprised by the remarkable words of the seemingly enlightened "Polish-born, French-speaking, English sea captain and novelist, Joseph Conrad," who wrote in his memoir: "A certain enormous buck nigger encountered in Haiti fixed my conception of blind, furious, unreasoning rage, as manifested in the human animal to the end of my days. Of the nigger I used to dream for years afterwards."[7] Chinua has expressed surprise in the failure of scholars to confront Conrad's racist views. For Chinua, "Conrad's fixation...is grounded quite firmly in that *mythology of imperialism* which has so effectively conditioned contemporary civilization and its modes of education." He went on to add this telling explanation:

> Imperial domination required a new language to describe the world it had created and the people it had subjugated. Not surprisingly, this new language did not celebrate these subject peoples nor toast them as heroes. Rather it painted them in the most lurid colors. Africa, being European imperialism's prime target, with hardly a square foot escaping the fate of imperial occupation, naturally received the full measure of this adverse definition. Add to that the massive derogatory endeavor of the previous three centuries of the Atlantic slave trade to label black people, and we can begin to get some idea of the magnitude of the problem we may have today with the simple concept: Africa is People.[8]

Chinua's views on imperialism and denunciations of colonialism applied more broadly beyond his native Igboland. At the end of the 1800s, under their King, Leopold II, the Belgians practiced the worst form of colonialism in Africa in the Congo. The king's very name was synonymous with colonial brutality against the native inhabitants of so-called Belgian Congo. In 1876, Leopold usurped the Congo as his private property to be exploited for his private gain. He personally controlled large areas of crown land and leased some areas to private companies on a profit-sharing basis. There was great demand for rubber in Europe's growing bicycle and later automobile industries. He made an enormous fortune from the Congo's rubber and ivory wealth. For tapping rubber, Africans received meager compensation, and their output was severely penalized as a "tax." Africans who failed to pay the tax in rubber, food or unpaid labor were "punished by flogging, chaining, mutilation, imprisonment, the burning of villages or death."[9] The king severed the heads of the Africans to thwart any domestic resistance, and cut off their hands as the penalty for failure to meet production targets. Such abuses enraged even the American novelist, Mark Twain.

Seeing beyond his local situation after having witnessed slavery in his own household and later being repulsed by it in his own country, Twain understood the odd link between European democracies and their use of savage force to enslave and destroy dark-skinned peoples in Asia and Africa and to steal their land. Twain denounced colonial violence and the rationalization of the "white man's burden"; that Europeans were justified in their violence against indigenous peoples of Asia and Africa in order to bring "civilization." "There are many humorous things in the world," Twain argued, "among them the white man's notion that he is less savage than other savages."[10]

Compelled by conscience, Twain wrote "King Leopold's Soliloquy," a forceful polemic, protesting the injustices of the Belgian king, who at the time had completed business arrangements with powerful American financiers to share in the looting of the Congo. In the United States, no publication agreed to print Twain's expose; so Twain gave it to the American Congo Reform Association to sell as a pamphlet "for the relief of the people of the Congo state." In 1904, the pressures of world opinion forced King Leopold to abdicate, and the colony was taken over by the Belgian government.[11]

Chinua Achebe considered it inaccurate to compare King Leopold's brutal practices with the relatively more "moderate" style of British colonialism. King Leopold's Congo exemplified the excesses of colonialism. To illustrate the king's mindset, Chinua, in one of his essays, quoted Leopold's own vernacular: "I am pleased to think that our agents....drawn from the ranks of the Belgian army...are animated with a pure feeling of patriotism; not sparing their own blood, they will the more spare the blood of the natives, who will see in them the all powerful protectors of their lives and their property, benevolent teachers of whom they have so great a need."[12] In short, to King Leopold II, the African was the "junior brother"; Africans were in their youth and needed Europe's guidance. Chinua Achebe had one fitting conclusion for "His Serene Majesty Leopold II in the Congo" and his colonialist exploits. It was purely and simply, like all other colonial enterprises, a "scandalous activity." Chinua recognized that the violence colonialism unleashed affected both victim and victimizer. It abused the rights of the colonized, and sapped the colonizer of a moral conscience. In characteristic understatement, Chinua noted that colonialism (and its elaborate structures of dispossession) was no "laughing matter."[13]

CHINUA ACHEBE: TEACHER OF LIGHT

NOTES

1. General Olusegun Obasanjo, *My Command: An Account of the Nigerian Civil War 1967-70* (London: Heinemann Educational Books, 1980), pp. 1-2.
2. Ronald Robinson et. al., *Africa and the Victorians : The Climax of Imperialism* (Cambridge, Cambridge University Press, 1996), p. 1.
3. P. J. Marshall, ed., *Cambridge Illustrated History: British Empire* (Cambridge, Cambridge University Press, 1996), pp. 7-9.
4. C. L. Innes, *Chinua Achebe* (Cambridge, Cambridge University Press, 1990), pp. 6-7.
5. Ibid., p. 7.
6. Achebe, "Education of a 'British Protected' Child," p. 52.
7. Chinua Achebe, *Africa Is People* (Washington, D.C., The World Bank, Presidential Fellow Lecture Series, 1998), p. 5.
8. Ibid.
9. Michael Tidy with David Leeming, *A History of Africa: 1840-1914* (New York, Africana Publishing Company), p. 147.
10. Clinton Cox, *Mark Twain, America's Humorist, Dreamer, Prophet: A Biography* (New York, Scholastic Inc., 1998), p. 183.
11. Ibid.
12. Achebe, "Education of a 'British Protected' Child," p. 52.
13. Ibid., p. 53.

CHAPTER 5

Primary School Days

In 1936, Chinua began kindergarten (locally called "infant
school") at St. Philip's Central School in the Akpakaogwe
section of Ogidi, a well-ventilated, T-shaped mud-building, where pupils cleaned the classrooms every Friday. As he
would note later, "Education at that level was completely in the
hands of native teachers, but the legacy of the unspared rod
remained, with just one small amendment. You were not walloped for laughing when a mistake was made but for making
it."[1] Saint Philip's was one of the best kindergarten schools in
the area. It had a soccer field, a choir, a farm, and mango trees
with emerald leaves that provided juicy fruit for the students
during the mango season.

After kindergarten, Chinua received his primary (elementary) education at the Ogidi Church Missionary Society (CMS)
Central School, which was run by Anglicans, and his first lessons were in his Igbo mother-tongue, in which he studied *Azu
Ndu* or "Fresh Fish," the CMS text for beginners. He learned to
read, write, and count in Igbo. In this beginner Igbo text, he also
learned religious discipline and the basic principles of practical

life. At age eight, he began to study English.[2]

Chinua spent two years in infant school and six years in primary school. He has noted that for some children, there was a preschool year in what was called Religious School, where they spent a year chanting and dancing the catechism:

Who is Caesar?

Siza bu eze Rom
Onye n'achi enu-uwa dum

(Caesar is the King of Rome
Who rules the entire world).

Who is Josiah?

Josaya nwata eze
Onye obi ya di nlo
Onatukwa egwu Chineke

(Josiah the infant king
Whose heart was soft
He also feared the Lord).[3]

Chinua was spared this preschool or daycare experience because he was precocious. Reverend Nelson Ezekwesili recommended that he be placed directly in kindergarten, where his first teacher was Alphonsus Ojukwu.[4] Although the first few days in school were difficult for him and he wept from fear and estrangement, he quickly adapted and became a star student. At home, he had additional daily doses of religion, reading parts of the Bible every morning and night. He also read the "chaotic literature" in his father's house: the ecclesiastical history in *The West African Churchman's Pamphlet;* discarded primers and readers inherited from his older brothers and sister, such as *A Midsummer Night's*

Dream; and his mother's *Ije Onye Kraist,* an Igbo adaptation of *Pilgrim's Progress.* At night, he read by the faint light of a flickering candle or by the timid glow of a hurricane lamp.[5]

The Second World War began when Chinua was completing his second year in primary school, what was called standard two. The remaining years of his primary school education took place against the "distant background" of the war. The events of the war hit closer to home when two white people and their assistants visited Chinua's school and conscripted his art teacher.[6]

During this period, Adolf Hitler, the antihero of World War II, was busy spreading his form of fascism. Although admired by some Nigerians, he was mostly despised and unpopular locally. There were a few naive young admirers, more fascinated and awed by Hitler's dominant presence on the world stage at the time than sensitive either to fascism's threat to world peace or to Hitler's capacity for evil. These gullible youths also believed that if Hitler was an enemy of the British colonialists, as they were themselves, then he deserved their local support.[7]

Chinua has described the climate of the times in relation to one of his schoolmates, a boy "who wrote a letter to Hitler," which was a "strange aberration." Nigeria, at the time, was loyal to Britain and did what it could to help the Allies. The headmaster, Mr. Okongwu, gave the boy severe flogging before the entire student body and reprimanded him as an "offspring of Satan." Headmaster Okongwu, "almost in tears," noted that the "boy was a disgrace to the British Empire, and that if he had been older he would surely have been sent to jail for the rest of his miserable life."[8]

The fight against fascism enjoyed considerable local support in Igboland. The people launched campaigns to increase palm kernel production for the war effort. Chinua recalled: "Our headmaster told us that every kernel collected in the bush would buy a nail for Hitler's coffin."[9] As the war continued, efforts mounted despite hardships. Supplies for the home and the schools dried up. Salt was rationed, and not a grain could be bought in the open market.

The song "Rule Britannia" retained its popularity, but the favorite song was "Germany Is Falling." Chinua recalled the lines:

Germany is falling, falling, falling
Germany is falling to rise no more.

If you are going to Germany before me
Germany is falling to rise no more
Tell Hitler I'm not coming there

Germany is falling to rise no more

If you are going to Italy before me
Tell Mussolini I'm not coming there

If you are going to Japan before me
Tell Hirohito I'm not coming there

When one enemy list was completed, students moved on to friends, whom they were naturally prepared to visit:

If you are going to England before me
Tell Churchill I am coming there

If you are going to America before me
Tell Roosevelt I am coming there

If you are going to Russia before me
Tell Stalin I am coming there

If you are going to China before me
Tell Chiang Kai Shek I am coming
there[11]

If you are going to Abyssinia before me
Tell Haile Selassie I am coming there.

This song was sung with evangelical zeal, almost like "Onward Christian Soldiers." Almost everyone in Igboland was convinced good would prevail over evil.

Chinua later reflected on what the world would have become like had Hitler won the war. In a poem titled "An 'If' of History," he narrated:

Just think, had Hitler won
his war the mess our history
books would be today. The Americans
flushed by verdict of victory
hanged a Japanese commander for
war crimes. A generation later
an itching finger pokes their ribs:
We've got to hang
our Westmoreland
for bloodier crimes
in Viet Nam![12]

For Achebe, history was never a tidy process of the victimizer always winning against the victims. In time, victims also have their day in the court of world opinion. In a continuation of the same poem, he explored the peril the world would have been in and the likely fate of leaders of the West had Hitler won:

But everyone by now must
know that hanging takes much more
than a victim no matter his
load of manifest guilt. For even
in lynching a judge is needed—
a winner. Just think if Hitler
had gambled and won what chaos
the world would have known. His

implacable foe across the Channel
would surely have died for
war crimes. And as for Truman,
the Hiroshima villain, well!
Had Hitler won his war
De Gaulle would have needed no
further trial for was he not
condemned already by Paris
to die for his treason
to France?... Had Hitler won,
Vidkun Quisling would have kept
his job as Prime Minister
of Norway, simply by
Hitler winning.[13]

There were happier moments in Chinua's primary school years. The peak was during times of festivities, especially the traditional festivals in Ogidi, which was only partially christianized when Chinua was growing up. Like all children, he looked forward to the *Nwafor Festival,* the main celebration of the traditional year that featured over a hundred masquerades of all kinds for eight full days.

There were also the Christian festivals: the big one was Christmas; the small one, Easter. There were two secular festivals that, as Chinua described it, livened up our Christian year: Empire Day on May 24 and Anniversary on July 27. May 24, as every school child knows, is the birthday of Queen Victoria. It was a major school event, and school children from all over the district would march in contingents past the British Resident who stood on a dais wearing a white ceremonial uniform with white gloves, plumed helmet and sword.[14] Empire Day celebrations took place at the provincial headquarters in Onitsha, and they would feature competitive games among the school children: tugs-of-war, sprints, long-jumps, and throwing the javelin. Only when Chinua was in standard three and ten years old was he judged old enough to make the trip to Onitsha to participate in Empire Day celebrations. He found Onitsha a "magical place," and the dawn view from a high road at a distance was "the river Niger glimmering in the sky," which "took a child's breath away."[15] Chinua felt sore for a whole week after his first initiation into the Empire Day events.

Both Chinua's academic and recreational schooling were reinforced at home. In later years, he recalled with humor the strict discipline, educational bent, and contradictory messages of his father's household. He wrote, "The Chinese did not invent wall posters for cultural education. My father did. Beside the picture of Miss Warner was a framed motto of St. Monica's School in blue letters. It said 'Speak True, Live Pure, Right Wrong, Follow the King.'"[16] Chinua had struggled to make sense of the juxtaposed English noun and verb in "Right Wrong." Such mixed messages from his father's colonial upbringing confused the youth. He reflected on this in amazing detail.

> My father filled our walls with a variety of educational material. There were Church Missionary Society yearly almanacs with pictures of bishops and other dignitaries. But the most interesting hangings were the large paste-ups which my father created himself. He had one of the village carpenters make him large but light wooden frames [into which] he pasted colored and glossy pictures ... from old magazines.... I remember a most impressive picture of King George V in red and gold, wearing a sword. There was also a funny-looking little man with an enormous stride. He was called Johnnie Walker. He was born in 1820 according to the picture and was still going strong. When I learnt many years later that this extraordinary fellow was only an advertisement for whiskey, I felt a great sense of personal loss.[17]

At age fourteen, Chinua was one of the few boys selected for enrollment at the Government College in Umuahia (GUC). This was considered a great achievement, for entrance into the school was very competitive, as the college had earned the reputation of being one of the best in West Africa. As a child raised by a strict father supporting his large family with a pension of two pounds sterling each month, Chinua did not do badly by local standards.[18] In primary school, he had been a well-behaved lad who was so bright that he was always at the top of his class in academic performance. His peers nicknamed him "Dictionary."[19] Not only did he excel in all his subjects- reading, writing, arithmetic, geography, nature studies, religious studies, and hygiene- he also had beautiful penmanship and the special gift of logic. Among his peers, only Aaron Ifekwunigwe came close to being a rival.[20]

During Chinua's rarefied boyhood years, he slept on wooden beds without mattresses, and had to fashion his own footballs, first from banana leaves and later by creatively tapping rubber trees to mold more durable forms. These were but minor hardships; Chinua's life was in fact quite privileged compared with that of most of his schoolmates because both his parents were literate.

He always looked forward to Sundays, when he would join in prayers and sang hymns with the local church congregation. Sundays were special not only because he attended church in both the morning and afternoon and dressed in his best Sunday khaki shorts and shirt and shoes, luxuries few of his peers possessed. On Sundays, his mother always cooked a special Sunday dinner, usually a meat stew served with rice or *fufu* (mashed yam) and servings of such tasty vegetables as *mai-mai* (spiced grinded bean) and plantain.[21]

Although Chinua liked school, his enthusiasm for it was marred by the corporal punishment meted out there. Students were flogged and whipped for the smallest infractions. Chinua also disliked the biased textbooks that often contained stories loaded with negative images of Africa. Some stories simply sounded strange. For example, the text of Chinua's *New Method Reader* began:

Once there was a wizard. He lived in Africa.
He went to China to get a lamp.[22]

Despite the shortcomings of his textbooks, Chinua became fond of stories. The more he read, the more he found himself absorbed in their form and content. As an avid reader, the future writer began to develop. Chinua also had periods of naughty behavior during his primary school days. One incident particularly stuck in his mind. One day, young Chinua decided to treat himself to some tasty *mai-mai* from the little market outside the school, but had no money and knew better than to ask his mother. So he decided to sell one of his arithmetic books. Unfortunately for Chinua Achebe, his mother happened to pass by the stall where he had sold the book, and she recognized it on display. Chinua had never seen his mother so angry. He received the whipping of his life that evening and, subsequently, had to go and retrieve the book. From that time on, he learned that school books were precious and privileged possessions.[23]

NOTES

1. Achebe, "Education of a 'British Protected' Child," p. 53.
2. Wren, *Achebe's World*, p. 13.
3. Achebe, "Education of a 'British Protected' Child," p. 55.
4. Ezenwa-Ohaeto, *Chinua Achebe*, p. 11.
5. Achebe, Hopes and Impediments, pp. 36-37.
6. Achebe, "Education of a 'British Protected' Child," p. 55.
7. Ibid., p. 55.
8. Ibid.
9. Ibid.
10. Ibid.
11. Ibid.
12. Chinua Achebe, *Beware Soul Brother: Poems* (London, Heinemann Educational Books, 1972), p. 16.
13. Ibid., pp. 16-17.
14. Achebe, "The Education of a 'British Protected' Child," p. 54.
15. Ibid.
16. Ibid., p. 53.
17. Ibid.
18. Awogbemila et. al., "Master Craftsman," p.18.
19. Achebe, "Education of a 'British Protected Child'," p. 54.
20. Ezenwa-Ohaeto, *Chinua Achebe*, p. 15.
21. Awogbemila, "Master Craftsman," p. 18.
22. Chinua Achebe, "African Literature as Restoration of Celebration" in *Chinua Achebe: A Celebration*, Kirsten Holst Petersen et. al. (eds) (Oxford, Heinemann Educational Books, 1990), p. 7 .
23. Authors' interview with Chinua Achebe, March 1995.

Government College, Umuahia

Government College, Umuahia (GCU) was one of the best colonial secondary boarding schools in West Africa. Achebe had the choice either of attending the popular CMS mission school Dennis Memorial Grammar School in Onitsha, or of attending GCU, which was 100 miles from Ogidi. The decision was not up to him however. It was a matter for his elders. His older brother, John, who had taken him in during his last year in primary school decided he should go to Umuahia, a choice Chinua believed was "absolutely right."[1]

It was common in those days to transfer to boarding school after primary school, and one obtained entrance only through extremely competitive exams. Chinua had indicated GCU as his first choice. Since he had passed the entrance exams, he was invited for an interview. It was at GCU that Chinua, at the age of 12, first came in close contact with a white man: William Simpson from Cambridge University, GCU's vice-principal.[2] Because of his strict manners and the broad powers he commanded throughout Igboland's educational system, everyone was in awe of this huge, odd-looking white man.

Chinua recalled his first encounter with Simpson as intimidating. He was nervous, and stood before him shaking. It was difficult to understand Simpson because of his British accent. Chinua arrived for his high school admission interview without prior acknowledgment of the letter Simpson had sent to him that stated, "Please acknowledge receipt." The young student had no clue as to what Simpson was talking about. Achebe stood before him, timid and confused, as Simpson thundered his accusations. The boy, who would one day teach Igbo society to the world in his novels, written in English and who would be one of this century's most able writers, did not at the time know the term "acknowledge." He had thought this was merely a fancy way of ending a letter. He recalled, "I thought I had failed."[3] He had not failed.

Chinua often wondered why the British colonial government in Nigeria had founded two elite boys' boarding schools after World War I. Whatever the reasons, they must have been part of the plan to advance British interests. Colonial authorities throughout the British Empire trained some "natives" to collect taxes, maintain law and order, and generally to help administer local affairs. The founding of GCU served these colonial objectives. Government College, Umuahia, opened its doors in 1929. Chinua noted that "an extraordinary English cleric, Robert Fisher, was appointed the founding Principal."[4] Fisher built the school's programs and reputation so much so that, at the time of his retirement eight years later, the name of the school was a byword for excellence.

Then came World War II, during which the colonial government shut down GCU and converted the buildings into a prisoner-of-war camp for Germans and Italians. Before the war ended, a policy shift returned the facilities to educational use. In 1944, GCU re-opened its doors to welcome Chinua Achebe's generation of students.[5]

Government College, Umuahia, was modelled after elite British public schools such as Eton and Harrow. The school ac-

commodated 200 students from forms I to upper VI (the equivalent of Grades 7-12), and Chinua's class consisted of thirty-two boys. The boys lived in dormitories called "Houses," which were named after famous landmarks, past and present teachers, and principals: Niger House, School House, Simpson House, Fisher House, Nile House, and Wareham House. Achebe was a resident of Niger House. The strict daily routine began with the wake-up bell at 5:35 A.M. Following morning prayers, at 6:00 A.M., the boys performed such morning chores as cleaning the dormitory, which ended at 6:30 A.M. After this, the boys took their bath and headed for breakfast, which began at 7:30 A.M. The boys began their classes at 8:00 A.M., which lasted until 1:45 P.M., and then had lunch 2:00 P.M.[6]

Despite this regimented environment, Chinua enjoyed the learning facilities at Umuahia and continued to earn distinction in that competitive environment, which fostered excellence among its group of bright boys. William Simpson shaped the school with a philosophy that discouraged students from excessive book-learning. He regarded excessive devotion to textbook work and cramming (which, in those days, passed for education in the colonies) as a real danger to young minds.[7]

Simpson, although himself a mathematics teacher, wanted students to extend their curiosity and develop their imagination by reading novels. So he devised the "Text-Book Act," a draconian rule that forbade the opening of any textbook after classes on three days of the regular week. This rule encouraged informal aspects of education, but it also fostered a spirit of suspicion, that someone was stealing precious moments of standardized learning from their young lives.[8]

After classes and lunch, the students rested, played games, washed, and were free until 7:30 in the evening, although not allowed to read their textbooks until bedtime. Students read novels, played ping-pong, or wrote letters, but were not allowed to read their textbooks. If they were caught reading textbooks, they were punished.[9]

Chinua Achebe read voraciously, consuming such English schoolboy staples as *Treasure Island, Tom Brown's School Days, Prisoner of Zenda, Gullivers Travels, Oliver Twist, and David Copperfield.* Although these titles did not reflect African realities, they fascinated the students. Chinua noted that "Even stories like John Buchan's *Prester John*, in which heroic white men battled and worsted repulsive natives, did not trouble us unduly at first. But it all added up to a wonderful preparation for the day we would be old enough to read between the lines and ask questions."[10]

The library at the Government College, Umuahia, was superior to that of most other schools. Achebe realized this only after he had graduated from university and began to teach at the Merchants of Light School in Oba, a few miles from Onitsha. There, to his amazement, he discovered that the school library had only few books and a Bible. Only then did he realize what a privilege the GCU library had been, filled with its rows and rows of books among which one could spend an entire afternoon. Besides the popular novels at GCU, there were also specialized books in physics, biology, chemistry; materials for the rest of the curricula and titles to meet the general reading requirement of one book per week. These books broadened students' minds beyond the narrow curricula.[11]

At GCU, Chinua had some teachers who were conventional in their approach and others who were innovative. Of the latter, there was an eccentric Australian, Charles Low, whom Chinua regarded as a genius. He often came to class unprepared, held totally unstructured classes, and sometimes wandered off the topic for most of the class period, after which he would state, "That's an important digression!" Much of Low's teaching, in fact, was digression, but it was enjoyable and highly instructive, and he greatly inspired his students to read and write. Mr. Low had studied Latin at Melbourne and the Latin and Greek classics at Oxford, and he occasionally recited poems and verse in class. He had a griot's memory and knew John Milton's *Para-*

dise Lost by heart. His students were often amazed by the speed with which he read books. Instead of teaching from the syllabus, he often came to class and asked his students to memorize ten lines from *Paradise Lost*. Like most other students, Chinua did not understand half of what he read in Milton, but he memorized the archaic lines of poetry and recited them the next day. He realized later that these assignments were integral to memorization training.[12]

Charles Low was most inspiring to his students because he involved them in his own creative writing, including his experimental plays and poems. One of his most memorable poems was about a social gathering that Simpson organized between the girls at the Women's Training College (WTC) and the senior boys at GCU. Chinua and his school mates were all excited because it was their first official encounter with the opposite sex. Inspired by the moment, Mr. Low wrote a poem called, "The WTC Are Here," which included the following lines:

> *Alone in the corner Egbuchulam glowers,*
> *Regretting how Oliphant wasted his hours.*
> *You don't learn from Durrell how to say it with flowers*
> *The WTC are here!*[13]

Egbuchalam was one of Chinua's Umuahia classmates, and the students were thrilled to see their experience distilled into poetry.

On another occasion Charles Low wrote a poem about a horse, which was used by travelling teachers who served remote schools in Igboland. The story in the poem was that of Mr. Otun from Calabar, a stout travelling teacher who, together with his wife, used the horse to inspect schools in Eastern Nigeria and the Cameroons. When the horse became sick, he gave it potassium permanganate, which failed to save the poor creature. Mr. Low wrote the poem in honor of the horse because it had rendered such great service to the cause of African education that it deserved proper burial. The poem was inscribed on the headstone of the poor animal's grave:

> *Here lies the gallant steed,*
> *Fallen to rise no more.*
> *Poor earthly laborer freed,*
> *By KMno4.*[14]

As befitting a good and humorous teacher who approached his students with care, Charles Low inspired the students to use their immediate experiences creatively in ways that stuck in their mind and fired their imagination.

Another teacher whom Chinua fondly remembered was Adrian ("Apple") P.L. Slater, from Canterbury, who instilled in him "respect for language." Slater drilled his students in basic logic and the scientific method, a demand not required of students even in his native England, and he required the students to read a dozen novels analytically every term or semester. A typical colonialist, he complained of being "sick and tired of African stupidity" and scorned the idea of an Africa in rebirth. A harsh man, he punished his pupils for the slightest infractions, using a wooden ruler on the knuckles. Though he set high academic standards, his students often exceeded his expectations.[15]

Barry Cozens was GCU's headmaster during part of the period Chinua Achebe was there. Despite a rigorous curriculum, Cozens noted that the boys at GCU achieved such high grades in their exams that it was an embarrassment compared with the student performances in his native England. Some Nigerian teachers, many of them from Rivers state, also taught at GCU at the time: Mr. W.E. Alagoa, a graduate of King's College, Lagos, taught chemistry and biology; Mr. I.D. Erekosima (nicknamed "John Bull") for lack of university opportunities, studied mathematics and physics at Yaba Higher College and taught mostly physics; and the late Mr. G.J. Efon, also taught physics.

Of the Nigerian teachers, Mr. W.E. Alagoa was one of the most impressive. Brilliantly resourceful, he often took students outdoors and carried out field experiments with them as part of his biology class. The students visited the school's gardens and the fish and crocodile ponds. Mr. Alagoa made Chinua and his classmates realize that science was not only a textbook activity but also a way of understanding their natural environment.[16]

So stimulating was the learning environment at GCU in those days, it was no wonder that many of Chinua Achebe's colleagues, including Nigeria's most accomplished poet, Christopher Okigbo, and authors Gabriel Okara, Elechi Amadi, Chukwuemeka Ike, and I.C. Aniebo, all went on to play major roles in the development of modern African literature.[17]

Much of the academic work at GCU and at other schools was geared toward passing the highly competitive Cambridge School Leaving Certificate Examination, designed at England's Cambridge University to administer to students both in Britain and in the colonies. To prepare for this exam, students and teachers had to follow the Cambridge syllabus beginning with the first year in high school throughout their next five years there. The teachers at GCU reduced the stress of preparing for the all-important final exam by preventing students from discussing the exam until a year prior to taking it. A school tradition was for all the exam-candidates to go on a compulsory picnic, without textbooks, on the weekend before the exam.[18] This was typical of the good balance between learning and leisure, discipline and creativity, that GCU fostered. Moderation was the norm, and the school heeded the adage that "all work and no play made Okafor a dull boy, and all play and no work made Okafor a mere toy." Students were encouraged to grow into well-rounded human beings.

Although Chinua enjoyed tennis, he was poor at sports. There were moments when the boys behaved naughty, as on another occasion when the boys engaged the girls of the Women's Training College in a netball march. Excited always by the co-educational gatherings, the young boys failed to keep their eyes on the ball and were even sometimes accused of "catching breasts instead of the ball."[19] Nevertheless, Chinua recalled that the balanced approach to life at Umuahia was a major factor not only in his overall development but specifically in his writing. Rather than dilute its strength, curriculum diversity and balance enhanced it.

Because Chinua was so bright and advanced during his first years, he, together with six other students in his class, was promoted directly to the third year. Chinua attended GCU from 1944 to 1947, a rather short period compared with the tenure of the average student. He, thus, took the School Certificate Examinations a year earlier than his peers, passed them with distinction, and obtained university entrance. He was selected as a "Major Scholar," a recognition with special benefits, in the first class entering at the new University College, Ibadan, in 1948.[20]

NOTES

1. Achebe, "Education of a 'British Protected' Child," p. 55.
2. Awogbemila, "Master Crafstman," p. 18.
3. Ibid.
4. Achebe, "Education of a 'British Protected' Child," p. 55.
5. Ibid., pp. 55-56.
6. Robert Wren, *Those Magical Years: The Makings of Nigerian Literature at Ibadan, 1948-1966* (Washington, D.C., Three Continents Press, 1991), p. 55; Authors' interview with Chinua Achebe, March 1995.
7. Achebe, "Education of a 'British Protected' Child," p. 56.
8. Ibid.
9. Ibid.
10. Ibid.
11. Wren, *Those Magical Years*, p. 57.
12. Ibid.
13. Ezenwa-Ohaeto, *Chinua Achebe*, p. 29.
14. Authors' interview with Chinua Achebe, March 1995.
15. Ezenwa-Ohaeto, *Chinua Achebe*, pp. 27-28.
16. Ibid., pp. 29-30; Wren, *Those Magical Years*, pp. 57-58.
17. Achebe, "Education of a 'British Protected' Child," p. 56.
18. Authors' interview with Chinua Achebe, March 1995.
19. Ezenwa-Ohaeto, *Chinua Achebe*, p. 29.
20. Wren, *Those Magical Years*, p. 58.

CHAPTER 7

University Life

C hinua's arrival in Ibadan, western Nigeria in 1948, marked a turning point in his life.[1] At the beginning of the century, higher education was beyond reach for most Nigerians. The British failed to establish universities in their African colonies either because they feared African nationalism or because they had doubts about African capacities to pursue university level education, particularly in the sciences. Their original approach was to propagate vocational education (such as carpentry, masonry, and brickmaking) for Africans. In fact, in 1925, a British government committee published what was known as a White Paper entitled *Educational Policy in British Tropical Africa* that endorsed and adapted for the African setting the vocational education that the American Negro leader Booker T. Washington so championed at Alabama's Tuskegee Institute.[2] Underlying all this was the British condescending attitude, reflecting their doubts about Africans' ability to pursue higher learning. At the time, only a few wealthy Africans could afford to attend university in Britain. Others enrolled in British universities as external students and obtained degrees the hard way.

After considerable protests by Nigerians, and after it became patently obvious that Africans were not only capable of qualifying for university but also of excelling at it, the British Labor government established the Elliott Commission under its namesake, Walter Elliott. Commission delegates traveled throughout West Africa, making inquiries, and chosing a suitable location to found a university for West Africa. The well-known biologist Julian Huxley was part of that Commission.[3]

Ibadan became a hub of learning for students who were to become the elite of an independent Nigeria. British professor Kenneth Mellanby established the campus in an abandoned military hospital and barracks in a section of Ibadan called Ele-iyele in 1947. The university opened its doors in 1948, modelled on premier British universities and designated as a college of London University in England. The college remained in Ele-iyele until the main campus was completed in 1952.[4]

Admission to University College, Ibadan (UCI) was extremely competitive for it served not only Nigeria, which had at the time a population of 32 million people but also its West African neighbors. Fortunately, for Chinua, GCU's high standards stood him in good stead. Achebe excelled in the entrance examinations and became one of the first students to enter Ibadan on a full scholarship. In science and in medicine, he attained *"Major Scholar"* status, becoming one of the *creme de la creme* in intellectual achievement. In any given year, there are only two selections for *Major Scholar* and about eight for *Minor Scholar* awards. Another measure of *Major Scholar* elitism was having a private room while other students shared.[5]

Although Chinua was good at chemistry and biology, he did not do well at physics. He also excelled in and tremendously enjoyed history and English. He, therefore, enrolled at Ibadan not fully enthusiastic about studying medicine. A prerequisite for the medical program included Latin, which he had not learned at Umuahia and was not eager to learn. This Latin requirement more or less decided his fate. Chinua stated: "It was clear to me early in the first year that I didn't want to do the grinding work in physics, or ultimately, in medicine. I didn't do well, I lost interest entirely." When he approached the dean about his desire to change professional direction, the dean reluctantly sent him to discuss the matter with the dean of arts.[6]

Chinua decided to switch professional direction to the arts. His interest in science had diminished, while his interest in history, geography, religious studies, and English literature was growing. During that time at Ibadan, English was just beginning to be regarded and taught as a foreign language. The early stages of a conscious nationalism were brewing.[7]

Changing professional tracks meant losing his science scholarship, so Chinua, with the help of his brothers, had to pay university fees for one year. His brother, John, who at the time was a low-ranking civil servant in Ibadan, had to cancel his own leave plans to earn enough for Chinua's fees.[8] This kind of family support, common at the time, was something Chinua never forgot. After paying for his first year, Chinua was able to obtain a scholarship to continue his studies.

At UCI, Achebe encountered several exciting professors, who influenced his writing enormously. Geoffrey Parrinder (religious studies), Paul Christopherson (head of the English department), James Welch (religion/philosophy), and Joyce Green-Garnier, then Miss Green, (English) were all well known in their respective field at the time. Parrinder was a lively and knowledgeable professor of religion. He came to Ibadan in 1949 and remained there until 1958. Before then, he had been a missionary teacher and had researched West African religions—a field in which he was pioneer—in Dahomey (Benin) and in the Cote d'Ivoire. Chinua and his friend Christian Chike Momah were the brightest students in Parrinder's class, and they always sat in the front row during his lectures, which gave them the flavor of various religious systems, including their own, thus introducing them to the comparative study of West African religions.[9]

Chinua was intrigued by James Welch, an eloquent preacher, in the religious studies department, who had been head of religious broadcasting at the British Broadcasting Corporation (BBC) in London, chaplain to King George VI, and principal of a theological college. He was a missionary in Nigeria in the 1930s, and had returned to Africa at the end of the World War II, serving as the director of education with the British government's East African Groundnut Scheme, which ultimately became a huge fiasco. Investing millions of pounds sterling, the British had tried to produce peanuts in Tanganyika (present-day Tanzania), but the entire project had failed.[10]

During his final year at Ibadan, Chinua had the opportunity to discuss student evaluations of the college with Professor Welch, then vice-principal. Welch's reply was instructive: "We may not be able to teach you what you want or even what you need. We can only teach you what we know."[11] Chinua admired Welch as a wise, honest, and conscientious teacher who never lost his calm even when facing difficult challenges.

In literature, Chinua encountered a curriculum rich in colonial caricatures of Africa and Africans. He read the novels of Joseph Conrad and Joyce Cary, which unabashedly illustrate their condescending European perspectives about Africa. The pictures these writers painted clearly excluded African perspectives and therefore served to reinforce colonial images and entrench the colonial enterprise. The books helped to defend the colonial order as a system of values and beliefs brought to deliver and enlighten the African. The books did not admit what George Orwell, the noted British writer, honestly acknowledged about colonialism and the imperial order in his essay "Rudyard Kipling"; that it was plainly a "money making concern" and therefore a "racket."[12]

These books depicted Africans as backward, primitive

peoples without history, living in tribal wards, and in a permanent state of internecine warfare, and without worthwhile civilizations. These books reinforced the European self-serving myth of Africa as the "heart of darkness," conveniently subscribed to by even such supposedly learned men as Hugh Trevor-Roper, Regius Professor of history at Oxford, who ignorantly even went to the extent of denying the existence of African history.[13] Colonial apologies though these books were, Chinua read them critically as sophisticated constructs of colonial propaganda to serve European empire building.

Chinua also read the works of William Shakespeare, John Milton, William Wordsworth, and other European literary luminaries. As much as he enjoyed the drama and human parallels in all of these European works, he did not see his people or his local circumstance featured in them. Africans were always insignificant characters; a servant, slave, houseboy, or sideshow savage. Chinua noted:

> I went to a good school modelled on British public schools. I read lots of English books there. I read "Treasure Island" and "Gulliver's Travels" and "Prisoner of Zenda", and "Oliver Twist" and "Tom Brown's School Days" and such books in their dozens. But I also encountered Ryder Haggard and John Buchan and the rest, and their 'African' books. I did not see myself as an African to begin with. I took sides with the white men against the savages. In other words I went through my first level of schooling thinking I was of the party of the white man in his hair-raising adventures and narrow escapes. The white man was good and reasonable and intelligent and courageous. The savages arrayed against him were sinister and stupid or, at the most, cunning. I hated their guts.[14]

It was not until much later, during his university years, that Chinua realized the subtle manipulations of the mind wrought by these books. He decided that Africans had to tell their own stories and present their own perspectives. Clearly, the Europeans would not do it for them.

The negative self-images that young Africans learned from these colonial books pushed Chinua in a direction toward becoming a writer. The urge to write came from his perspective as a critical reader. He began experimenting with writing early but with no immediate role models; his avocation as a writer was that of a self-starter. He noted, "At 10, I was interested in stories. I didn't really know that stories were made up by people. I thought stories like that of the sky and forest (recounted on moonlit nights at home) were just there and nobody put them there."[15] This declaration unambiguously demonstrated that the future writer came from an oral tradition. This strange recognition that people wrote stories made him declare "that if they could write stories, so could I,"[16] and what better endeavor than to tell stories and put words in the mouths of his own people, the Africans.

University College, Ibadan, crystallized the making of Chinua the writer. He had written prose in secondary school, but he had not made up his mind to become a writer. His English writing and poetry classes at university gave him confidence, and his impulse to write came from a pioneering sense that the many terrible and false representations of Africa needed correcting.

Achebe reminisced:

A time came when I reached the appropriate age and realized that these writers had pulled a fast one on me! I was not on Marlowe's boat steaming up the Congo in [Conrad's] Heart of Darkness. I was one of those strange beings jumping up and down on the river bank, making horrid faces. Or, if I insisted on the boat-ride, then I had to settle for that "improved specimen," as Conrad sarcastically calls him, "more absurd than a dog in a pair of breeches trying to make out the witchcraft behind the ship's water-gauge."[17]

Achebe realized that "stories are not innocent: they can be used to put you in the wrong crowd, in the party of the man who has come to dispossess you."[18] This important discovery—that there was something dehumanizing in the way stories about Africa were told—led Chinua to conclude that Africans had to break their silence and begin to narrate their own stories.

NOTES

1. Wren, *Achebe's World,* p. 13.
2. Edward Berman, "Christian Missions in Africa" in *African Reactions to Missionary Education* (New York, Teachers College Press, Columbia University, 1975), pp. 11-12.
3. Achebe, "Education of a 'British Protected' Child," p. 56.
4. Wren, *Those Magical Years,* p. 18.
5. Ibid., p. 58.
6. Ibid.
7. Ibid., p. 60.
8. Ibid., p. 58.
9. Ibid., pp. 59-63.
10. Achebe, "Education of a 'British Protected' Child," p. 56; Authors' interview with Chinua Achebe, March 1995.
11. Jerome Brooks, "Chinua Achebe: The Art of Fiction," *The Paris Review,* vol. 35, no. 133 (Winter 1994-1995), p. 147; Wren, *Those Magical Years,* p. 66.
12. George Orwell, *A Collection of Essays* (Garden City, New York, Doubleday Anchor Books, 1954), p. 126.
13. Achebe, *Hopes and Impediments,* p. 2.
14. Chinua Achebe, "African Literature as Restoration of Celebration," in Kirsten Holst Petersen et. al., eds., *Chinua Achebe: A Celebration,* p. 7.
15. Awogbemila, "Master Craftsman," p. 15.
16. Ibid.
17. Achebe, "African Literature," p. 7.
18. Ibid.

CHAPTER 8

The Making of a Writer

Even without African role models, Chinua was determined to be a writer. In his years at Ibadan, he struggled with the pretenses of colonial education. The English department at Ibadan did not make matters easy; that Chinua and some of his contemporaries would someday become writers never crossed the minds of their professors. The very notion would have amused them.

Chinua had started scribbling creative works in private essays, stories, and even poems. Some of these stemmed from his reactions to stories about other people and places; some came from his own observations at the cultural crossroads which he was himself experiencing, and others concerned the colonial caricatures of Africans. He recognized early that there was a danger in not having your own stories, and noted later that "there is that great proverb, that until the lions have their own historians, the history of the hunt will always glorify the hunter."[1] He added, "Once I realized that, I had to be a writer. I had to be that historian. It's not one man's job. It's not one person's job. But it is something we have to do, so that the story of the hunt will also reflect the agony, the travail, the bravery, even, of the lions."[2]

Chinua's first public literary effort was to enter a competition that the English Department sponsored that required students to write a short story over the long summer vacation. He had never written fiction before, but he decided to try his hand and to submit his story for the departmental prize. After evaluation, no prize was awarded because no entry was considered up to standard, but Chinua's piece was given an honorable mention. He took this as an accolade, knowing the emphasis on excellence at Ibadan. As he noted, "Ibadan in those days was not a dance you danced with snuff in one palm. It was a dance you danced with all your body. So when Ibadan said you deserved mention, that was very high praise."[3]

Joyce Garnier-Green, a Victorian lady who taught Tennyson, had organized the competition. Chinua approached her to ask for criticism of his submission. She kept postponing her response, saying she would explain in the course of the term, but Chinua kept begging her for an explanation. Finally, she said, "I read your short story again, and I don't think there's anything wrong with the form."[4] That was all that Chinua learned about writing stories from the English department; however, he kept writing. Even without the prize, the students started their own journal, *The University Herald,* which the university funded but the students controlled. In contrast with its campus rival, *The Bug,* a satiric publication, *The Herald* was serious and literary and featured essays, poems, and stories. Chinua was recruited to the editorial committee and elected as chief editor in his third year. He published four of his short stories in *The Herald*— "Polar Undergraduate," "In a Village Church," "Marriage Is a Private Affair," and "Dead Man's Path"; all were later published in his short story collection *Girls at War and Other Stories.*[5]

One of Chinua's memorable experiences at Ibadan was hearing one of his poems read over Radio Brazzaville of Congo, perhaps the most powerful station in the whole of Central and

West Africa in those days. The poem was a limerick that Chinua had published in *The Herald,* but which, in his more mature years, regarded as a "silly, stupid and nonsense kind of poem."[6] Sir Eugene Millington-Drake, a tall, gaunt English poet who travelled around the world reading English poetry and a real performer, read the limerick:

> *It's about a young man in our hall,*
> *Who said because he was small,*
> *His fees should be less,*
> *Because he ate less,*
> *Than everybody else in our hall.*[7]

Millington-Drake went on to comment that Chinua was himself very small. The limerick gave Chinua his first international publicity.

When Chinua graduated, he had no clear plans about his future profession, but in those days jobs were not difficult to find. He returned to Ogidi, where a friend who was teaching mathematics at the Merchant of Light school in Oba convinced him to come and teach English.

While Chinua taught there, Professor Welch tried to get him a scholarship to attend Trinity College, Cambridge, for graduate studies, but that did not work out. Subsequently, Welch exerted his influence to have him hired by the Nigerian Broadcasting Corporation (NBC), which included a number of former British Broadcasting Corporation (BBC) staff.[8]

Chinua edited scripts, speeches, and short stories in the "Spoken Word" or "Talks Department," which clearly fitted his tastes. He developed the skill of commissioning and editing short stories that proved valuable in his professional development as a writer and editor. With events moving quickly in newly independent Nigeria, he was soon promoted and became director of External Broadcasting.[9]

In 1957, with another Nigerian colleague, the late Bisi Onobanjo, editor of *Radio Times* and former governor of Ogun state, Chinua was granted a scholarship to visit London and to study for several months at the BBC staff school. He carried along the draft of his first novel *Things Fall Apart*. His Nigerian colleague constantly urged him to show his manuscript to Gilbert Phelps, an instructor and novelist at the BBC school. Initially shy, Chinua eventually agreed. Phelps reacted unenthusiastically when he received the manuscript, as do many established writers with the work of a novice. Later, after reviewing the work, he became the first person to remark to Chinua, "I think this is wonderful. Do you want me to show it to publishers?" Achebe said, "Yes, but not yet," since he had decided that the form of the novel was not yet right. In that first draft, Chinua realized he was covering too much ground in attempting to document the saga of three families. He decided to take the manuscript back to Nigeria.[10]

The neophyte novelist returned to Nigeria, revised the work, and sent it back to a typing agency in England that he had seen advertised in the *Spectator* during his London stay. They acknowledged receipt and requested a fee of thirty-two pounds for two copies, which Chinua forwarded by British postal order. Weeks and months passed, and Chinua wrote several letters, but there was no reply. He became disillusioned. Luckily, his boss at the broadcasting house, Mrs. Angela Beattie, a very stubborn English woman, volunteered to help when she visited England. When she turned up at the London office one day and asked, "What's going on?" They were surprised. They replied that the manuscript was sent but customs returned it. She asked for their dispatch book, which they did not have, and instructed them to send the typed manuscript back to Chinua in the next week. A brief period thereafter, Achebe received the typed manuscript. There was only one copy, and no apologies were given for what happened.[11]

Achebe sent the typed manuscript to Heinemann, Gilbert

Phelps's publishers. They had never seen an African novel and were not sure what to do with it. They sent it for review to Donald MacRae, an economics professor at the London School of Economics and Political Science, who has just returned from "those places." MacRae turned out to be a humane and learned man, whom Chinua would later get to know. Heinemann said that MacRae's report was the shortest they had ever received on any novel, eleven words: *"This is the best novel I have read since the war."*[12]

This is how *Things Fall Apart*, Chinua's first novel was launched. The initial 2000 hardback copies were printed without any editing, on June 17, 1958. They all sold like "hot yams" and vanished from the bookstores. The British writer C.P. Snow reviewed it in the *Times Literary Supplement* and many other favorable reviews appeared. Alan Hill, the editor at Heinemann, went against prevailing prejudices and launched a substantial paperback edition that sold for twenty five pence and did exceptionally well. *Things Fall Apart* has since sold more than three million copies in the UK edition alone, more than eighteen million copies worldwide, and has been translated in almost all of the world's forty major languages, including *Thai*, spoken in Southeast Asia, a new frontier where it is doing particularly well. Today, the novel is regarded as a classic of world literature.[13]

The publication of *Things Fall Apart* marked one of the most significant literary events in the development of modern African literature. Its instant success launched Heinemann's *African Writers Series*, which provided the main outlet for most of the continent's writers and has since published more than 100 titles. Heinemann used the revenues from *Things Fall Apart* to subsidize the publication of its other African titles. Although Chinua was honored to be appointed founding editor, his genius and much of his valuable time was employed in reading and commenting on even the most terrible manuscripts. The series, however, provided a great service to the modern literary development of Africa. Alan Hill, who took risks with Chinua's first book, was later made a Commander of the British Empire (CBE) for bringing into existence a body of literature considered among the most significant in this century.[14]

NOTES

1. Brooks, "Chinua Achebe," p. 146.
2. Ibid.
3. Ibid., p. 148.
4. Wren, *Those Magical Years*, p.59.
5. Ibid., p. 59-60.
6. Authors' interview with Chinua Achebe, March 1995.
7. Ibid.
8. Ibid.
9. Ibid.
10. Ibid.
11. James Currey et al., "Working With Chinua Achebe: The African Writers Series," in Kirsten Holst Petersen and Anna Rutherford, eds., *Chinua Achebe*, p. 149; Brooks, "Chinua Achebe," p. 151.
12. Ibid., p. 150.
13. Ibid., pp. 150-51.
14. Ibid.

CHAPTER 9

Man of the Family

In 1958, Christie Chinweifenu Okoli, a student studying drama at the University College, Ibadan, took a vacation job at the Nigerian Broadcasting Service (NBS) in Enugu, capital of eastern region. Christie and a colleague were annoyed to learn that another student was earning more than they were, so they brought the matter to the controller for redress. Christie and the controller were attracted to each other at first sight. The controller was Chinua Achebe.[1]

Although Christie's family originated from Umuokpu, a section of the Igbo town of Awka, where Chinua's mother came from, Christie was born in Port Harcourt and grew up in Calabar and Enugu, where she stayed with her parents while on vacation. She was the youngest child in a family of five daughters and one son. Her Igbo name "*Chinwe*" means "my *chi* or personal deity owns me," which further signifies that her *chi* was to guide and shape her destiny.

Christie already had a boyfriend, a medical student at University College, Ibadan. Although Christie had reformed his social image and curbed his alcoholism sufficiently to have earned thanks from one of his relatives, still she had reservations about their future and about his family.[2] Christie was brought up immersed in traditional Igbo values which emphasized marrying into a "right family"" and a "good family." Somewhat later, when Christie discovered that her boyfriend was from Rivers State and had not been fully honest about his family background, their relationship deteriorated.

Chinua's reliability, inner strength, and simple lifestyle impressed Christie. She also was pleased to learn that his mother came from her hometown. Having been both brought up in traditional Igbo society, origins mattered a lot. But as Christie recalls, "When I met him, there was nothing at all to suggest I would end up with him."[3]

While Christie was recuperating in hospital after an appendectomy in 1959, she was pleasantly surprised by a visit from Chinua, who came to wish her well and brought her gifts and magazines. Chinua's compassion and kindness strengthened their relationship, which blossomed into love.[4]

On September 10, 1961, the two were married at the Chapel of the Resurrection on the UCI campus. Several of Chinua's friends since his Umuahia days attended. Christian Chike Momah, Chinua's best friend and classmate, served as best man. Sam Nwoye presided over the reception ceremony of the marriage. The poet Christopher Okigbo, then living in Ibadan as representative of Cambridge University Press and writing poetry, also attended.[5]

In the early years of their marriage, insecurities required attention. Christie recalled, "The only time we had a [major] disagreement was during the earlier period of our marriage. As a new wife I had to pack his clothes in a bag whenever he had to travel. There was a time I saw a little note accompanying a new pair of socks."[6] The note obviously got her jealous, as she suspected him of having an affair. As trust grew, Christie became more comfortable and confident with the marriage. As she pointed out, "There was never a time that I confronted a woman because I saw her with my husband. I did not bother to ransack his belongings if he returned from a trip."[7]

As in many marriages, the early years were rough, and both worked hard to build trust and to make compromises on the demands made by each other's careers. In those years, Christie sometimes felt Chinua spent more time working on a novel than sharing his love with her. Such feelings of resentment generally vanished when both made efforts to soothe hard feelings.[8]

The young couple's relationship matured and deepened as their insecurities evaporated. They became more caring for each other, especially after children entered the scene. In time, the couple had four children, two girls and two boys: Chinelo (a daughter born in 1962), Ikechukwu or Ike (a son born in 1964), Chidi (a son born in 1967), and Nwando (a daughter born in 1970).[9]

The Achebes instilled in their children the values of education, honesty, hard work, and respect for Africa's cultural heritage. The children are all adults now and demonstrate those qualities. Chinelo has followed her father's path and published a collection of short stories, *The Last Laugh and Other Stories*. She studied English at the University of Kent in England and continued to complete her masters in comparative literature at the University of Guelph in Canada. She is married, lives at present in New York, and has two daughters, who are spoiled by the grandparents.

Ike received a doctorate in history from Cambridge University after completing his first degree in English at the University of Kent. In appearance, he is a replica of his father. He is bright but reserved; and presently lives in Washington, D.C. He feels strongly Nigerian, and visits it often. Chidi trained as a medical doctor at New Hampshire's Darmouth College and at Harvard (vindicating a dream his father could not realize), and presently lives in Cambridge, Massachusetts. He is lively and entrepreneurial, and has a knack for scientific curiosity even as a child, when he would dismantle and assemble toys, and carry out experiments, including mixing chemicals in the family bathroom. Nwando received a doctorate in history at the University of

California in Los Angeles, where she got married and presently lives with her daughter in Williamsburg, Virginia where she teaches at the College of William and Mary. A theatrical person during childhood endeared to the performing arts—drama and dance, she also has a serious scholarly orientation.

Christie Achebe obtained her doctorate in education at the University of Massachusetts in 1976, took a lectureship in education, guidance, and counseling at the University of Nsukka in Nigeria throughout the eighties, and now teaches psychology with her husband at Bard College. Chinua was always considerate about his wife's career development. While Christie was working on her thesis, he would take the children to Enugu to allow their mother to complete her work. Christie remarked, "This is what I say in terms of appreciating somebody's understanding of your lifestyle, the way you bring in your best and he supports it."[10]

Christie Achebe has described her relationship with her husband as mature and beautiful: "It doesn't mean you didn't quarrel or that you don't have differences or long spells of not talking to each other. But I will say our relationship has really matured into a very profound relationship and with a lot of respect and caring on his part for me [and vice versa, her for him]."[11]

For Chinua, Igbo tradition offered useful guideposts for a marriage. "The Igbo are not starry-eyed about the world. Their poetry does not celebrate romantic love. They have a proverb which my wife detests, in which a woman is supposed to say that she does not ask to be loved by her husband as long as he puts out yams for lunch every afternoon."[12] Chinua noted this was a "drab outlook for the woman,"[13] but it reflected the pragmatism of the Igbo. Though not undervaluing love, a man had to be responsible and to provide for his family but, above all, to cope with the trials of marriage. As Chinua further noted, "Marriage is tough; it is bigger than any man or woman. So the Igbo do not ask you to meet it head-on with a placard, nor do they ask you to turn around and run away. They ask you to find a way to cope. Cowardice? You don't know the Igbo."[14]

The solid foundation on which the marriage was built was not only trust, but caring and understanding. As Christie has further noted, "I will say some of the insecurities I heard some women complaining about how their husbands treat them, I don't get them, and I cannot even fathom that sort of thing is possible between human beings. Chinua is very caring, understanding, and very busy. He travels most of the time, but any time he comes back and I am with him, he sort of makes up the time he missed. In a nutshell, it is a very rich relationship between us. I don't have the option to choose, but if I had to, I would go back to him."[15]

Unlike many writers or artists, Chinua has not gone through bouts of alcoholism, stormy affairs, court battles for handsome settlements, and endless divorces. He is a devoted and responsible, family man. In his stories and in his life, the family features as primary anchor. When he travelled, he made sure that his wife and children were not stranded without financial assistance, always making sure they had some support to fall back on. He puts the yams on the table. He would also telephone and write, and encourage his wife to assume backup responsibilities wherever it was practicable.[16]

When Chinua was busy writing, Christie often prevented visitors from disturbing him, but he did not mind interference from his family. Christie noted:

> When he is writing he doesn't talk much. Perhaps it is because when you are thinking... you don't want to diffuse it by talking. As I can remember, the book he spent [more] time on than others [was] *Arrow of God*. That is a profound book for him. In the early years of our marriage, he spent a lot of time on the book more than on me. But writing is not a chore to him. He started... *Anthills of the Savannah*, many years ago but he left it and later he picked it and finished it in no time."[17]

There may be truth to the saying that besides every great writer stood a great home editor. Christie has been the first reader for Achebe's works. Christie has remarked, "I don't intrude while he is trying to create. Once he finishes writing, I become the first to read the manuscript.... Sometimes, I read as he writes. I reserve my comments till he finishes. ....He does listen to suggestions. But by and large, I agree with what he writes and says."[18]

Christie and Chinua have recreated a substitute home base at their bungalow at Bard College, a place where the whole family can gather during holidays. Chinua still gets his *onugbu*, his favorite bitter leaf soup, with his *fufu* or *pounded yam*, whenever the ingredients can be found. Surrounded by New England deer, rabbit, squirrel, wild turkey, the couple enjoy the wildlife but enormously miss Nigeria, the source of Achebe's creative inspiration. They fill lonely moments, outside of their teaching, with reading and writing, grading papers, conversations with and visits by friends, attending ceremonies, and movies.

NOTES

1. Soji Omotunde, "Our Relationship Is Profound," *This Week*, 152 (1989), p. 21.
2. Ezenwa-Ohaeto, *Chinua Achebe*, pp. 67-68.
3. Omotunde, "Our Relationship," p. 21.
4. Ezenwa-Ohaeto, *Chinua Achebe*, p. 68.
5. Wren, *Those Magical Years*, p. 65.
6. Awogbemila, "Master Craftsman," p. 23.
7. Ibid.
8. Omotunde, "Our Relationship," p. 21.
9. Innes, *Chinua Achebe*, 1990, pp. xv-xvi.
10. Omotunde, "Our Relationship," p. 21.
11. Ibid.
12. Achebe, "Education of a 'British Protected' Child," p. 52.
13. Ibid.
14. Ibid.
15. Omotunde, "Our Relationship," p. 21.
16. Ibid.
17. Ibid.
18. Ibid.

CHAPTER 10

A Great Fearful Thing: The Nigerian Civil War

The Nigerian civil war, also known as the Biafran War, blazed from July 6, 1967 to January 12, 1970.[1] It was the worst of times for Nigeria's inhabitants. A history of ethnic rivalry made worse by British policy of divide and rule; sponsorship of authoritarian tribal rulers, such as the Emir of Sokoto; siphoning of resources through unequal trade; resulted in political upheavals that led to two *coups d'état* and the subsequent civil war. Without the British, Nigeria's ethnic groups would probably not have united as one country. For before the British, Nigeria was composed of different city states, empires and kingdoms, such as Gobir and Kano of Hausaland; Ife and Oyo of Yorubaland; and Umuahia and Umuofia of Igboland, places only loosely associated through trade and sometimes war.

The causes of the civil war have been ascribed to ethnicity religion, and economics. The ethnic element is that the British brought together into one nation three large ethnic groups with irreconcilable differences. This created an uneasy coexistence. The religious explanation is that the traditionalism of the Islamic north clashed with the modernism of the southwest and southeast, where Western education held sway. The economic explanation is that the north and southwest went to war against the southeast (the future secessionist state of Biafra) because oil, which had been newly discovered at the time, was concentrated in the Delta areas of the southeast and so were Nigeria's ports. In actuality, the war was a consequence of all three causes.

When Nigeria achieved political independence from Britain on October 1, 1960, it was governed at the federal level by an alliance of two parties: the Northern People's Congress (NPC), representing the Hausa/Fulani of the north; and the National Council of Nigeria and the Cameroons (NCNC), representing the Igbo of the southeast. The Action Group (AG), representing the Yoruba of the southwest, was excluded. Dr. Nnamdi Azikiwe, an Igbo and leader of the NCNC, became president of the federal republic of Nigeria; and Alhaji Sir Abubakar Tafawa Balewa, a Hausa/Fulani and deputy leader of the NPC, was the first federal prime minister. Sir Ahmadu Bello, the *Saurdana* (traditional ruler) of the Hausa/Fulani state of Sokoto, was then leader of the NPC and premier of the northern region; Dr. Michael Okpara, an Igbo, was premier of the Igbo region of the southeast. Chief Samuel L. Akintola, a Yoruba, was premier of the southwest.

The Yorubas were largely excluded from the power-sharing within the federal government because their party, the Action Group (AG), was in the opposition. The Action Group (AG) was headed by Chief Obafemi Awolowo. The Yoruba-dominated Action Group therefore rallied support among ethnic minorities in the southeast and the north, respectively challenging the hegemony of the Igbo NCNC and the Hausa/Fulani NPC in those regions. The federal government fought to halt this. In 1962, the government gerrymandered Awolowo's political base in the southwestern region by creating the midwest state in the region of Benin city to empower the non-Yoruba minorities there and appointed Chief Dennis Osadebay as premier.[2]

Also in 1962, Chief Akintola, premier of the Yoruba-dominated southwest and deputy leader of the AG, broke ethnic ranks with Awolowo and aligned himself with the Hausa/Fulani north by forming the western branch of the north's NPC party. He did this partly to increase his power and partly to further Yoruba interests. The Hausa leader, Sir Ahmadu Bello, supported Akintola, hoping to substitute him for Okpara, his difficult NCNC ally in the east. With Bello's backing, Akintola won the elections in the Southwest. Balewa wanted to reduce ethnic tensions by broad representation in federal power sharing from all regions.[3] Akintola's victory spurred protests in the southwest.

With the turmoil, Nigerian intellectuals and writers played significant roles. The writer Wole Soyinka, Awolowo supporter and later to be a Nobel Laureate, is alleged to have prevented an announcer at Ibadan's Radio Station, then main voice of the southwest region, from broadcasting Akintola's taped speech and to have replaced it with a damaging speech. Protests in the southwestern region led by Chief Awolowo took the form of violent civil unrest, which included petrol-fuelled houseburnings and widespread pyromania known as *Operation Wetie* (i.e., operation wet it).[4] Chief Awolowo and eighteen Yorubas were arrested by the federal government, charged with treasonable felony and illegal importation of arms into Nigeria.[5] They were jailed in 1963.[6] While in prison, most Yorubas continued to idolize and agitate for Awolowo and rejected Akintola's authority. Against this unstable background, the north-southeast coalition began to weaken.

Controversies over the 1962 and 1963 censuses, the 1964 elections, and the north's growing power, based on its allegedly inflated population numbers, heightened tensions.[7] Population figures from the first controversial census was superseded by the contentious, but more acceptable second census report, which showed the north as having 29 million people. This was more than half of the country's population of approximately 47 million, and it guaranteed the north the largest share of federal power.[8] Although the north covered vast territory, its population was considered small and sparse. Southerners joked that the northerners of the savanna grassland had inflated their population figures by counting their cattle and goats; northerners joked that the Southerners in the forest zone counted in trees as part of their population.

At the time of these events, Chinua Achebe was director of external broadcasting for the federal national radio, Radio Nigeria. His generation of university graduates and intellectuals exhibited high moral energy and idealism. They wanted to see Nigeria soar to be a shining star in Africa and among the nations of the world. Sharing these views were many well-educated and well-trained officers in the Nigerian army, many of whom had been classmates of intellectuals like Achebe. These professionally diverse groups shared hopes for building a better country and distaste for political laggards among the federal politicians. The Nigerian poets, Christopher Okigbo and John Pepper Clark (fondly called "J.P."), were, for example, classmates and friends with Major Emmanuel Ifeajuna, later to be a key figure in the first Nigerian coup.[9] At the time, Okigbo, Clark, Achebe, Soyinka, and the coterie of graduates from University College Ibadan were all vocal critics of the bribery, materialism, flamboyance and generally corrupt politics which were emerging in independent Nigeria. Although educated under colonialism, these young intellectuals detested the political system and the anti-social, capitalist greed that accompanied it. Many, as a result, became attracted to socialist politics.[10]

When the first postindependence civilian federal government, led by Sir Abubakar Tafawa Balewa, began to show signs of gross incompetence, Achebe's generation of intellectuals and army officers took notice. Achebe has described the mood of those times, as follows:

> something nastier had seized hold of all of us. The six year-old Nigerian federation was falling apart from the severe strain of regional animosity and ineffectual central authority. The

transparent failure of the electoral process to translate the will of the electorate into results at the polls led to mass frustration and violence. While [South]Western Nigeria, one of the four regions, was going up literally in flames, the Nigerian Prime Minister was hosting a Commonwealth Conference to extricate Harold Wilson from a mess he had got himself into over Rhodesia. But so tense was the local situation that the visiting heads of government had to be airlifted by helicopter from the Lagos airport into a secluded suburb to avoid rampaging crowds. Nigeria's first military coup took place even as those dignitaries were flying out of Lagos again at the end of their conference. One of them, Archbishop Makarios of Cyprus, was in fact still in the country.[11]

Nigeria's first military *coup d'état* of January 15, 1966 was staged against this background. The coup leader Major Chukwuma Kaduna Nzeogwu, an Igbo, expressed the high idealism of the army on radio in Kaduna at the dawn of the coup:

> Our enemies are the political profiteers, swindlers, men in high and low places that seek bribes and demand ten percent, those that seek to keep the country permanently divided so that they can remain in office as Ministers and VIPs of waste, the tribalists, the nepotists, those that make the country look big for nothing before international circles.[12]

On the eve of the coup, Achebe and J.P. Clark were at a meeting of the Society of Nigerian authors held in the Lagos Exhibition Center. Clark had borrowed a pre-publication copy of Achebe's fourth novel, *A Man of the People*, which satirizes political corruption in Nigeria and prophesies a military coup.[13] J.P. Clark remarked, "You are a prophet. Everything in this book has happened except the coup." By next morning, the coup, too, had come true, and some Nigerians read the prophetic novel as proof that Chinua had prior knowledge of the coup and therefore had helped plan it. Chinua recalls: "Critics called me a prophet but some of my countrymen saw it differently. My novel was proof of complicity in the first coup."[14] He further explains:

> I intended it to scare my countrymen into good behavior with a frightening cautionary tale. The best monster I could come up with was a military coup d'état which every sane Nigerian at the time knew was far-fetched! But life and art had got so entangled that season that the publication of the novel and Nigeria's first military coup happened within two days of each other![15]

On the night of the coup, Wole Soyinka was in hiding in his University of Lagos office, near a canoe anchored in the lagoon behind the university. As a dissident intellectual, Soyinka had attacked the government over the radio after the fraudulent election of 1962, and he had mobilized a violent "people's revolt" in southwestern Nigeria favoring Awolowo over Akintola. Soyinka was targeted by the federal government in a "scorched-earth program for the southwest, a program to sweep cleanly the southwest of 'dissident intellectuals' and trade unionists" who disagreed with the government's political line.[16]

On January 16, 1966, the morning following the coup, Achebe had no idea of what was happening. He arrived at Broadcasting House to find the place surrounded by soldiers. He detoured and went home. Later, that Sunday morning, he received a phone call from Broadcasting House that drunken, armed soldiers were searching for him to test which was stronger, his pen or their gun.[17] The offense of his pen was the foretelling of the coup in *Man of the People*.

Nigeria's first military *coup d'état* resulted in multiple assassinations. The coup plan was to send non-Hausa soldiers to the north to eliminate northern leaders; non-Yoruba soldiers to the southwest to eliminate Yoruba leaders; and non-Igbo soldiers to the southeast to eliminate Igbo leaders. In keeping with this plan, in the southwest, the Yoruba Chief Akintola was killed by troops led by the Igbo Captain Nwobosi. In the north, Sir Ahmadu Bello, the Sardauna of Sokoto and Premier of the northern region, was killed by troops led by the Igbo Major Chukwuma Kaduna Nzeogwu. In Lagos, then capital of Nigeria, Major Emmanuel Ifeajuna, an Igbo, arrested Prime Minister Balewa and his neighbor, Finance Minister, Okotie-Eboh; took them to a highway; and shot them.[18] He also eliminated other superior officers but spared the army commander, Major General Umunakwe Aguiyi-Ironsi, an Igbo, who rallied loyal troops and the police to restore order. These killings eliminated all the regional premiers, except those of the southeast (Azikiwe was on sick leave in England, and the southeastern premier, Dr. Michael Okpara and Chief Osadebay, may have received advanced warning and gone into hiding). In addition, the fact that most of the coup plotters were Igbos created the interpretation that the coup was an ambitious Igbo plot to dominate and govern Nigeria.[19] This public perception brought untold horror to the majority of Igbos, some of whom were innocent, but who later suffered the most genocide prior to and during the Nigerian civil war.

In this tense atmosphere and power vacuum, General Ironsi, also an Igbo and the highest ranking military leader in the federal government, assumed the role of head of the nation and proclaimed a unitary state, unifying the civil service and abolishing the regions. This caused further unrest. He proposed a military constitution which aroused fear among northerners, who saw themselves overwhelmed by the better-educated southerners who stood to penetrate and dominate the northern civil service.

More than other writers, Okigbo and J.P. Clark became deeply involved in the drama leading up to and after the first Nigerian coup. When Nzeogwu's fellow coup plotters in Lagos, led by Major Ifeajuna, did not arrest Major General Ironsi, who rose to take power, Ifeajuna fled to Ghana. Major Ifeajuna was smuggled by Okigbo and Clark, who disguised him as a woman, across three countries to reach Ghana. Later, they brought him home to a hero's welcome, but, in Lagos, Ifeajuna was arrested and jailed.[20]

On January 18, 1966, General Ironsi appointed military governors to the four regions of the former federation: Lt.-Colonel Odumegwu Ojukwu represented the eastern region; Lt.-Colonel F.A. Fajuyi, the southwestern region; Lt.-Colonel David Ejoor, the midwestern Region, and Lt.-Colonel Hassan Katsina (son of the emir of Katsina), the northern region. Lieutenant Colonel Yakubu Gowon, a northerner from Plateau State, was made chief of staff and therefore head of the army.[21] The new military regime of General Ironsi did not last long either. The assassinations of Prime Minister Balewa, the Sardauna, and other leaders caused anti-Igbo riots in the North. The Sardauna of Sokoto was idolized in the North as a cultural and religious icon. His assassination created a severe northern backlash of revenge killings against the Igbo. Chinua noted:

> In the bitter atmosphere of the time, a naively idealistic coup proved a terrible disaster. It was interpreted with plausibility as a plot by the ambitious Igbo of the [South] East to take control of Nigeria from the Hausa-Fulani north. Six months later, northern officers carried out a revenge coup in which they killed Igbo officers and men in large numbers. If it had ended there, the matter might have been a very tragic interlude in nation-building, a horrendous tit-for-tat. But the northerners turned on Igbo civilians living in the north and unleashed waves of brutal massacres which Colin Legum of the Observer first described as a pogrom. It was estimated that 30,000 civilian men, women and children died in these massacres. Igbos were fleeing from all parts of [federal] Nigeria to their homeland [in the southeast].[22]

The second Nigerian coup took place against these background of events. It was led by northerners and was directed against the Igbos. Among the Igbo officers assassinated was General Ironsi, after which Colonel Yakubu Gowon, the army chief of staff, was chosen as head of state, because he appeared ethnically neutral. Gowon was a Christian from the minority Angas community in a predominantly Muslim region (middle belt plateau).[23] To dilute the power of the regions, especially that of the Igbos in the southeast, Gowon proposed dividing Nigeria's four regions into twelve states and placing the country's oil resources in the hands of the non-Igbo minorities in the southeastern Region.

Gowon's authority was not recognized by the Igbos, especially by the Igbo leader Colonel Ojukwu, because of Gowon's northern background and the prevalent prejudice in the north against the Igbos then. Igbos became more suspicious, according to Chinua, in light of the massacre of thousands of Igbos in the north, where they had migrated to pursue business opportunities and to take up civil service jobs, because they had better western education. Gowon's idea of a unitary Nigeria with 12 states was unsatisfactory to Achebe and to Igbos because it was seen as a weakening the regional power of the Igbos.

The news of the massacres of the Igbos in the north in May 1966, initially sanitized as "riots" in government pronouncements, came to Achebe's knowledge as a stab in the conscience. Chinua and Christie Achebe had attended a party at J.P. Clark's house on the University of Lagos campus on the eve of the killings. As news of the massacres came in next day, Chinua returned to Clark's house to confirm the news, only to discover Clark's home was padlocked. His friend had fled to his village without conveying the horrendous news to Achebe.[24]

In the days following Gowon's assumption of power, it became clear to Chinua from mounting news accounts that a terrible tragedy was being unleashed against the Igbos. Accounts of atrocities against Igbos in the north spread like wildfire and became difficult for his family to bear. News of southeastern

Nigerian army officers being slaughtered, of Igbo civilians being gunned down in the north and other places, of children being set on fire in locked houses, of pregnant Igbo women being
raped, accelerated. Perplexed by the troubling news, Chinua
and Christie saw that their hopes of a united Nigeria were being
dashed almost right before their eyes.[25]

NOTES

1. Obasanjo, *My Command*, p. 1.
2. James Obioha Ojiako, *13 Years of Military Rule 1966-79* (Lagos: Daily Times of Nigeria Ltd., 1979), pp. 1-3.
3. Ibid.
4. Ezenwa-Ohaeto, *Chinua Achebe*, p. 108.
5. Ojiako, *13 Years of Military Rule*, p. 3.
6. Ibid.
7. Ibid.
8. Ibid., p. 1; p. 212.
9. Personal phone conversation with Chinua Achebe, September 2000.
10. Wren, *Those Magical Years*, p. 5.
11. Achebe, "Chinua Achebe," p. 14.
12. Ezenwa-Ohaeto,*Chinua Achebe*, p. 109.
13. Wren, *Those Magical Years*, p. 66.
14. Achebe, "Chinua Achebe," p. 15.
15. Ibid.
16. Wole Soyinka, *The Man Died* (Ibadan, Spectrum Books Limited, 1988), p. 161.
17. Achebe, "Chinua Achebe," p. 15.
18. Ali A. Mazrui and Michael Tidy, *Nationalism and New States in Africa* (Exeter, New Hampshire: Heinemann Educational Books,1984), p. 239.
19. Achebe, "Chinua Achebe," p. 14.
20. Wren, *Those Magical Years*, p. 5.
21. Ojiako, *13 Years of Military Rule*, p. 7.
22. Achebe, "Chinua Achebe," p. 14.
23. Mazrui, *Nationalism and New States*, p. 242.
24. Ezenwa-Ohaeto, *Chinua Achebe*, p. 114.
25. Ibid., p. 115.

CHAPTER 11

The Biafran Tragedy

On Sunday morning, at the height of the violence, one of Achebe's staff members at Broadcast House called him at his home in Turnbull Road to say that soldiers were looking for him, and that he should flee. Achebe, confused because he had no criminal record and was unsure as to why the soldiers would be after him, telephoned Victor Badejo, director general of NBC, to confirm this. Badejo advised him to take Christie and leave immediately.[1] Fortunately, Achebe followed this advice, because when the soldiers finished searching for him at Broadcast House, they came to his residence and found it already vacated. He had taken Christie, who was pregnant, and their first two children, Chinelo and Ikechukwu, into hiding, and was preparing to send them to his hometown in southeastern Nigeria. He hid at the home of Frank Cawson, the British council representative. When he received a telephone call there asking for him, Achebe decided it was time to leave Lagos.[2]

Achebe, worried that Christie and the children might be stopped at the military road blocks set up in certain parts of the country to identify Igbos, sent his family by ship to Port Harcourt. Many years later, Achebe recalled the sorry state of southeastern refugees in the ship; their weariness, their spitting and vomiting, the general unsanitary conditions in the ship, and the disparaging remarks of their former Lagos neighbors, who quipped, "Let them go, food will be cheaper in Lagos."[3] The food aboard was cooked and served from large, unhygienic drums. The journey to Port Harcourt was long and hard. When Christie Achebe reached Port Harcourt, the trauma and arduous journey had taken their toll: she suffered a miscarriage.[4]

While in Lagos, Achebe met with Victor Badejo. Badejo, surprised that Achebe was still around, admonished him, "Life has no duplicate! You must go away immediately!"[5] Badejo's concern and the ominous phone call at Frank Cawson's, together with worries about the safety of his family, persuaded Achebe to leave by road. Luckily, by following a circuitous route, he was able to avoid all the trouble spots and make it safely to his home town of Ogidi, where he was reunited with his family and his worried mother.[6]

During this period, in August 1966, Achebe stayed in his hamlet of Ikenga in Ogidi. Too anguished to work, he read newspapers to keep in touch with the unfolding tragedy. The seeming insensitivity of some of his compatriots troubled him. He cites especially an article by Tai Solarin, a well-known intellectual, who advocated that Hausa become Nigeria's national language, because the massacres of Igbos would not have taken place if all Nigerians spoke Hausa instead of English. Solarin's logic was that the majority's language should rule. Achebe's view was that many of the Igbos did in fact speak Hausa well but little English, and uniting Nigeria required sensitivity to its diverse peoples and cultures. He reprimanded Solarin, "In your grand design for Nigeria, do not discount human beings; it will get us nowhere."[7]

Following news of a lull in the violence, Christie Achebe bravely returned to Lagos to the great worry of her writer husband and managed to retrieve their personal belongings, including some of Chinua's books and manuscripts, and returned to

Ogidi safely to his great relief.[8]

The flood of Igbo refugees may have opened spaces in departed areas for other Nigerians to fill, but, in Igboland in 1967, the military governor, Lt. Colonel Emeka Ojukwu, was overwhelmed by the throngs of unemployed returnees. The *Aburi Accord*, signed in January 5, 1967 by Gowon and Ojukwu, in Aburi, Ghana, had aimed to resolve national political tensions. It contained provisions for reorganization of the Nigerian army, under a Supreme Military Council to be chaired by a commander in chief and head of the Federal Government. Decisions affecting the whole country were to be made by the Supreme Military Council. Upon return from Aburi, Colonel Ojukwu claimed the agreement was that the regions should move slightly apart to enable them to co-exist. General Gowon, the commander in chief, disagreed with this interpretation and argued that the way Ojukwu was interpreting the Accord would end Nigeria as a single country. So the Accord fell apart when Gowon returned to Lagos and was advised by some members of his government to abandon it. Colonel Ojukwu, however, stuck to his interpretation of the Accord, and the slogan, *"On Aburi, We Stand,"* became his popular proclamation.[9]

While Achebe was in Igboland, Chukwuemeka Ike, a schoolmate of Achebe's and a fellow writer, persuaded him to start an institute of African studies at the University of Nigeria, where Ike was registrar. Achebe's poet friend, Christopher Okigbo, wanted to participate in the Institute, but some members of the staff objected.[10] A mood of impending national doom still prevailed, and the unwieldy march of national political tensions still sizzled uncontained.

Nigerian intellectuals were deeply entangled in the dramas leading to the Civil War. Christopher Okigbo's poem, "Come Thunder," for example, had included this prophetic verse:"

> *Remember, O dancers, the lightning beyond the earth...*
> *The smell of blood already floats in the lavender-mist*

> *of the afternoon.*
> *The death sentence lies in ambush along the corridors of*
> *power;*
> *And a great fearful thing already tugs at the cables of*
> *the open air*[11]

Okigbo had also captured the somber mood of the times:

> *The arrows of God tremble at the gates of light,*
> *The drums of curfew pander to a dance of death;*[12]

J.P. Clark suggests in a poem that Soyinka, in an effort to avert war, shuttled off to the southeast to meet with Okigbo and tell him that the Yorubas of the Western Region would support a Biafran invasion because they were also unhappy with the domination of the north and were eagerly waiting to join the rebellion.[13]

The civil war broke out on May 30, 1967, when the Igbos in the southeast under Colonel Emeka Odumegwu Ojukwu declared Biafra an independent state with Enugu chosen as its capital. Biafra also had its own national currency. The Igbos had made this secessionist move with the promise from Chief Obafemi Awolowo in the southwest that the Yorubas would follow suit. The plan was if the southeast and southwest broke away from the Nigerian federal union, the federal government would not be able to fight a war on two fronts. Awolowo, however, failed to honor his pledge, and the secession proved a nightmare for the Igbos. Awolowo, in fact, became the minister of finance of the federal government during the civil war. The Igbos interpreted this as a sign of bad faith on the part of a Yoruba leader, and trust was further eroded between the two ethnic groups. The Yorubas using superior federal military power, in alliance with the north and other Nigerian groups, and supported by the British forced the Igbos back into the federal union after a period of three years.

In late July 1967, in the early days of the civil war, Soyinka did in fact visit Biafra but it is unclear whether the motives ascribed in Clark's poem were the reason for his mission. Biafran intelligence tracked Soyinka from the moment of his entry into Enugu, and summoned him to the Military Police Headquarters on Abakaliki Road for interrogation. A large Biafran crowd had gathered shouting that the "saboteur" be given to them for instant mob justice. Bernard Odogwu, director of Biafran Military Intelligence, did not believe that Soyinka was a "saboteur," but nevertheless questioned him about his mission.[14] The following is Odogwu's recollection:

"Mr. Soyinka, What brings you to Biafra? And do you realize that you are in enemy territory and subject to being treated as a spy?"

Soyinka answered, "Hell, I am in Enugu, and I come to see my friend Colonel [Emeka] Ojukwu. You see, I was away on tour in the United States and Europe when the civil war started. While abroad, some mutual friends of ours (Colonel Ojukwu and himself) could not believe that Emeka would allow the Nigerian crisis to degenerate into a shooting war and asked me to get in touch with him on my return. When I got back to Nigeria, I heard several stories about all sorts of destruction in the [South]east— Hotel Presidential destroyed, this and that place destroyed, Ojukwu on the run, and things like that, so I decided I had better come down and see things myself, and to give Emeka the full length of my tongue if I saw him. Emeka should have shown more maturity, you know. We all must do something urgently in the interest of our nation and people."

"What nation are you referring to Mr. Soyinka?" Odogwu probed.

"Nigeria, of course. Which else?"

"You mean you don't recognize the existence of Biafra? But in any case don't you think you have come rather too late in the day? Where were you when some of your colleagues, Achebe, Okigbo, Ekwensi and Nzegwu to name a few, were being pushed out of Nigeria? What did you do?"

"Yes, I have come to tell Emeka off. I will do the same to Gowon when I get back to Lagos. It is really a pity and very sad that our fatherland [Federal Nigeria] is being destroyed by chaps of our own age and we have not tried hard enough to do something about it. We must try and stop them before it is too late."[15]

While Odogwu was about to tell Soyinka he had not answered his questions, Soyinka interrupted, "Where is Christopher Okigbo? Is it possible that I could see him?"[16] Odogwu informed him that Okigbo was in the heat of battle at the war front. Just then, though, Okigbo surprised them both by appearing at the door in full battle gear. The friends hugged each other and, to the astonishment of the military policemen, broke into a jig. When this subsided, Okigbo and Soyinka argued about the merits and demerits of the on-going civil war, and why Okigbo was fighting when he should have used his influence to prevent it. At the end of their conversation, Soyinka said, "I recognize the fact that you people had gone through hell in the last year and that most of us in Nigeria were guilty because not many people had the guts to speak up when the damage was being done." Then he continued, "I hope that pretty soon we shall be able to find some sort of peace formula to unite the country once again."[17] He went on to say that he hopes that the outcome of the war would not result in the erection of national borders around Biafra that would require him to use a passport when next he wanted to visit Enugu. As they parted fondly, Okigbo said with an air of finality, "Well, dear Wole, I hope we meet again, but if not, I hope this parting was well made. Keep the flag flying high as always."[18]

Soyinka subsequently met Colonel Emeka Ojukwu and Colonel Victor Banjo. Banjo, a Yoruba, had been detained in the southeast after the first Nigerian coup, when Ironsi became the head of state. Ojukwu later released Banjo from detention and accommodated him at the state lodge to the envy of others. Ojukwu's ambition was for Biafra's secession to succeed; Banjo's was to rule the rest of Nigeria. Their compact was that Ojukwu would support Banjo in his southwestern expedition to topple Gowon, after which Banjo would reciprocate by granting Biafra full autonomy and sovereignty. Banjo, together with Adewale Ademoyega, the only other Yoruba among the rebels, initially succeeded in leading an army across southern Nigeria to Benin City. He planned to take over Ibadan and Lagos further up the road, and eventually reached as far as the borders of the southwest in Yorubaland at Ore.[19]

The campaign was Banjo's chance to "liberate" the south from two enemies: the federal military government, and his own commander's Igbo-controlled, ill-conceived Biafra as well. It was a chaotic time of loose loyalties. Neither Banjo nor Ademoyega— nor Soyinka, if he had choice—would have handed the conquest to Ojukwu. They all regarded him as a crass reactionary. "Soyinka, according to J.P. Clark in a poem, was: *picked up like a rabbit on the road/In daytime, en route to proclaim another kingdom.* He was jailed by the federal government, and proclaimed nothing."[20]

Clark became a staunch supporter of the national government and a united Nigeria. During this time, he detested intellectuals like Wole Soyinka for their seemingly ambivalent role.

Banjo and Ademoyega did not succeed in their westward push to capture the seat of power in Lagos, and Banjo tried to appease two opposing camps by shuttling between Biafran headquarters in Enugu, his headquarters in Benin, and the national government headquarters in Lagos. Suspicions arose in Biafra about his Lagos dealings which led to the general feeling that he was a saboteur. He was subsequently arrested by Ojukwu, indicted for treason, and executed along with Emmanuel Ifeajuna.[21]

During the war, external governments gave arms and money to both sides, thereby exacerbating the conflict. Great Britain and the Soviet Union, for example, supported the federal side, especially with arms; whereas Charles de Gaulle's France supported Biafra. When France recognized Biafra, some of its former colonies, Cote d'Ivoire and Gabon, for example, did so as well. Portugal also supported Biafra. The United States, however, was officially neutral, although in reality, because of its transatlantic loyalties, it sided with Britain. Haiti under Papa Doc recognized Biafra and sent a most flamboyant letter, offering sentiments "from the pinnacle of the Negro race."[22] Tanzania under Julius Nyerere and Zambia under Kenneth Kaunda also recognized Biafra. In addition, many grassroots organizations supporting Biafra such as "Save Biafra Associations" were formed in many Western countries.

Achebe's reflections about Nigeria were ones of "profound disappointment." How could the federal government renege on its obligations to protect its Igbo citizens who, in Achebe's words, were "hunted down and killed in the most savage manner, innocent civilians in many parts of northern Nigeria?"[23] Achebe also found it hard to forgive outside meddlers and their oil interests. He noted, "The demise of Nigeria was only averted by Britain's spirited, diplomatic and military support of its model colony. It was Britain and the Soviet Union which crushed the upstart Biafran state. At the end of the 30-month war, Biafra was a vast smouldering rubble. The cost in human lives was...staggering..., making it one of the bloodiest civil wars in human history!"[24]

The Biafra war, or Nigerian civil war, proved to be the worst tragedy of Nigeria's modern history. At first, Biafran forces fought vigorously and triumphantly, but later the capture of Port Harcourt by federal forces cut off a major supply artery to the outside world and tilted the equation in favor of the federal forces. Over two million civilians were killed, with Igbos suffering the greatest casualties, as they were starved into submission. As an Igbo, Chinua Achebe's sympathies were naturally for the Biafran cause, and he never regretted his involvement. He was a key player in Biafra's Ministry of Information, working with its minister at the time, Dr. Eke Ifegwu. Ifegwu had assembled a strategy group (in which Achebe was a key player) to brainstorm periodically about what type of society Biafra should be and what was to be done once the war was over. Around the middle of the war in 1968, the Biafran head of state, Col. Ojukwu, was not happy with the work of the minister of information. He therefore summoned Achebe to the state house and appointed him chairman of the National Guidance Committee, which was to brainstorm and draft the national strategy. Caught between the minister of information and the state house and, after coming to the conclusion that more could be achieved with Ojukwu, Achebe assumed the job at the state house to develop a strategy for the future of Biafra. The end result was the formulation of the Biafran ideological tract: *The Ahiara Declaration*. The *Declaration* was a populist and democratic statement of principles which governed the Biafran revolution. It emphasized self-reliance, social justice, accountability, and African nationalism.

During the war, Achebe also worked hard as a fundraising ambassador to further Biafran interests around the world, especially in Britain and the United States. He publicized federal Nigeria's atrocities and attempted to rally international support for Nigeria's renegade region of Biafra. During those turbulent times, Achebe took great risks to get into a derelict Super Constellation airplane and fly to pro-Biafran Lisbon, Portugal, where the plane was allowed to land. He would then transfer to ordinary commercial aircraft and fly to such destinations as London, England.[25]

The civil war ended on January 12, 1970. The war turned Biafra into a grim wasteland: Dead bodies were everywhere; bombed houses and offices, paralyzed electric lines, broken water pipes, collapsed wells, sewage stench, kwashiorkor children with rust-colored hair and other symptoms of widespread malnourishment. Homes and infrastructure had to be reconstructed.

The University of Biafra at Nsukka, bombed and looted during the war, resumed its old name of University of Nigeria, and had to undergo substantial rehabilitation.[26]

For Achebe, the war also had huge personal costs. His apartment was bombed during the second month of the war, but luckily the lives of his wife and children were spared. He lost several relatives and friends. Christopher Okigbo, a major in the Biafran army and close friend, was killed in battle near Nsukka very early in the war in 1967. Achebe had collaborated with Okigbo in running Citadel Press, a little publishing house they had established in 1966 in the "safe stronghold of Enugu."[27] Achebe's trauma over Okigbo's death is expressed in his tribute essay, "Don't let him die," recording the reaction of his eldest son, Ikechukwu Achebe, when he relayed the "terrible news" of Okigbo's death to his family.[28]

Achebe stayed long enough to receive whatever possible reprimand or punishment was due him for renouncing Nigeria during the war. He lived in Nsukka for some years, attempting to rebuild his life and to reflect on the traumas of the war. Fortunately, the federal government under General Gowon was in a mood of national reconciliation, and it proclaimed a general amnesty for the secessionists. In September 1972, Achebe left Nsukka for a teaching appointment at the University of Massachusetts, Amherst, arranged by his writer friend, Professor Harvey Swados, who had visited him in Biafra. Swados died of a heart attack shortly after Achebe arrived in Amherst. Achebe was deeply anguished; life then seemed like a sequence of tragedies.

Achebe stayed four years at Amherst and then spent another year at the University of Connecticut before returning home. Achebe described those teaching experiences then as "by far my longest exile ever from Nigeria, and it gave me time to reflect and heal somewhat."[29]

NOTES

1. Ezenwa-Ohaeto, *Chinua Achebe*, p. 116.
2. Ibid.
3. Ibid., p. 117.
4. Ibid.
5. Ibid., p. 118.
6. Ibid., p. 119.
7. Ibid., p. 120.
8. Ibid., p. 120-123
9. Ibid., p. 120-121
10. Christopher Okigbo, *Labyrinths: Poems* (London: Heinemann Educational Books Ltd.), 1971, p. 66.
11. Ibid.
12. Wren, *Those Magical Years*, p. 5.
13. Ibid.
14. Bernard Odogwu, *No Place to Hide: Crises and Conflicts inside Biafra* (Enugu, Nigeria: Fourth Dimension Publishing co., Ltd.) p. 23.
15. Ibid., p. 23-24.
16. Ibid., p. 24.
17. Ibid., p. 25.
18. Ibid.
19. Wren, *Those Magical Years*, p. 5.
20. Ibid., p. 7.
21. Ibid.
22. Personal Conversation with China Achebe, September 2000.
23. Achebe, "Chinua Achebe," p. 15.
24. Ibid.
25. Currey, "Working with Chinua Achebe," p. 155.
26. Ezenwa Ohaeto, *Chinua Achebe*, p. 156.
27. Achebe, *Hopes and Impediments*, p. 114.
28. Ibid., p. 116.
29. Achebe, "Chinua Achebe," p. 15.

PHOTOGRAPHS

Chinua Achebe as Director of Voice of
Nigeria, Lagos, 1964. *Photo: with permission of
Chinua Achebe*

Christopher Okigbo, Chinua Achebe and Alex Olu Ajayi c. 1959
Photo: with permission of Chinua Achebe

University Herald Editorial Board, 1952-3 from left to right, Chinua Achebe, Chukwuemeka Ike, Mabel Segun, D. Oforiokuma, Agu Ogan and Akio Abbey. *Photo: with permission of Chinua Achebe*

Chinua Achebe receiving honorary doctorate
at Dartmouth College, Hanover NH, 1972.
Photo: with permission of Chinua Achebe

Harvey Swados with Chinua Achebe in
Biafra, 1969. *Photo: with permission of Chinua
Achebe*

With the Nigerian Press: Mrs. Christie Achebe (far left) and Chinua Achebe
(on wheelchair), 1999. *Photo: with permission of Nduka Otiono and* This Day
newspapers

Nwando Achebe and her daughter and Chidi Achebe, August 1999
Photo: with permission of Nduka Otiono and This Day *newspapers*

Chinua Achebe receiving the First Nigerian National Creativity Award
from the Minister of Culture and Tourism (August 1999).
Photo: with permission of Nduka Otiono and This Day *newspapers*

Lunch at the Presidential Villa, Abuja. Front row (right to left); Mrs Christine Achebe, President Olusegun Obasanjo, Chinua Achebe, and Vice-President Atiku Abubakar. Back row (left to right): Dr. Menkaya, Dr. Chuba Okadigbo, Dr. Nwando Achebe, Dr. Dele Cole and Dr. Ike Achebe
Photo: with permission of Nduka Otiono and This Day *newspapers*

Pesident Obasanjo welcoming Chinua Achebe at the Presidential Villa
Photo: with permission of Nduka Otiono and This Day *newspapers*

Chinelo Achebe and children
Photo: with permission of Ike Achebe

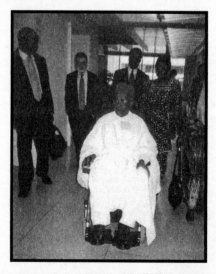

After World Bank lecture, co-authors, Tijan Sallah and Ngozi Okonjo-Iweala with two World Bank Africa Region Vice-Presidents, Calisto Madavo and Jean-Louis Sarbib accompanying Achebe and wife.
Photo: with permission of Latjorr (Gabriel) Ndow

CHAPTER 12

Heart of Light: The Novelist as Teacher

Chinua Achebe is the author, co-author, or editor of seventeen books. Among these are novels, short stories, poems, children books, essays, anthologies, and political commentaries. The novel, however, is the genre for which he is most famous, having published five of them: *Things Fall Apart (1958)*, *No Longer at Ease (1960)*, *Arrow of God (1964)*, *A Man of the People (1966)*, and *Anthills of the Savannah (1987)*.

What distinguishes Chinua Achebe's writing from other African writers, however, is not its quantity for he is not prolific, but its quality. His novels are deceptively simple and accessible and so richly interlaced with Igbo proverbs that they have the rare classical elegance of biblical parables. South African Nobel Laureate Nadine Gordimer has described him as "gloriously gifted with the magic of an ebullient, generous, great talent," as a "novelist who makes you laugh and then catch your breath in horror."[1] The diverse international praise for Achebe's literary gifts are simply too vast to enumerate. Author John A. Williams, for example, noted that "Achebe is a gifted and sensitive writer; his books reveal the subtle horrors of colonialism as well as the indomitable spirit of West Africa to survive it."[2] The *New York Times* observed that "much of Achebe's considerable power...is achieved through his fine sardonic sense of the comic."[3] Novelist Margaret Atwood states, "Achebe is a magical writer—one of the greatest of the twentieth century."[4] Novelist Michael Ondaatje comments, "He [Achebe] is one of the few writers of our time who has touched us with a code of values that will never be ironic. This great voice."[5] Harvey Swados summed up Achebe's literary achievements, writing that he was "quite simply one of the best novelists now alive."[6]

Things Fall Apart (1958), Achebe's first published novel, derives its title from the W.B. Yeats's poem "The Second Coming," which the Irish poet drew from Christian doctrine that the return of Jesus Christ would herald the end of world history, followed by an apocalypse, and the eternal reign of God. Yeats adapted that Christian view of the world to his own, using the "Second Coming" to signify the chaotic and cataclysmic changes of the pre- and post-World War II era, which for him signaled the imminent return of Christ. Yeats's poem reads in part:

> *Things fall apart; the center cannot hold;*
> *Mere anarchy is loosed upon the world,*
> *The blood-dimmed tide is loosed, and everywhere*
> *The ceremony of innocence is drowned....*[7]

Achebe's novel fits the broad inspiration of Yeats's poem, so it was not surprising that he used a line from the poem as the title for his book. *Things Fall Apart* features the far-reaching social changes set in motion by Africa's tragic encounter with Europe. "Community innocence" was lost. African traditional values and beliefs, despite their resilience, were transformed by the introduction of Christianity. Colonialism's divide and rule policy pitted neighbors and relatives against each other. And, more damaging, the African psyche was so disturbed that Africans after colonialism developed an ambivalent self-confidence.

Things Fall Apart revolves around the culture of Umuofia, a traditional Igbo village. The story dramatizes the disintegration or falling apart of the community, partly because of its internal weaknesses and its naive villagers and partly because of the sheer power and craftiness of the European. The name, Umuofia, means "children of the forest or bush" or simply "bush children," a depiction Achebe uses to portray the isolated but settled, orderly, and coherent life of traditional Igbo society, untouched by European culture. The tragic hero of the novel, Obi Okonkwo, is introduced as a strong personality, a skilled wrestler, and good farmer, who has proven himself admirably in the village, far away from the reputation of his effeminate father, Unoka, who was a loafer and a hedonist. Achebe deliberately gives his hero the name Okonkwo, after "*nko,*" the Igbo's busiest and most intense market day, perhaps to demonstrate this character's intensity and inner strength. Okonkwo's entire life, he tells us, is dominated by fear of failure and weakness.[8]

In that male-dominated society where age, hardwork, and masculinity are respected, Okonkwo distinguishes himself as a strong man and earns respect, even among the elders, and is awarded two titles. Fortunately, in Igbo society merit is rewarded so that, "when a child washed his hands, he could eat with kings."[9] Okonkwo, however, has character flaws. He is a "man of action," unquestioningly loyal to tradition, who demonstrates great personal impatience and inflexibility towards unsuccessful people and towards the unfamiliar. His entire life is achievement-oriented.

After he has become successful, he inadvertently kills a kinsman, and is for seven years exiled to another village, Mbaino. Upon his return, Okonkwo discovers that all aspects of Igbo traditional life in his village are under attack. European missionaries have established a church, and colonial administrators have astutely taken control of public administration. Okonkwo tries to mobilize his people, using that popular rallying cry "Umuofia united," to oppose the white man, but discovers that many of his own people have betrayed the old ways and have converted to the white man's religion. Even his own son, Nwoye, attracted by the "gentleness" of the new religion, has joined the Christians. His people are no longer united. Things had fallen apart. Achebe described the context in Obierika's reply to Okonkwo's question, "Does the white man understand our custom about land?"[10]:

> How can he when he does not even speak our tongue? But he says that our customs are bad; and our brothers who have taken up his religion say that our customs are bad. How do you think we can fight when our own brothers have turned against us? The white man is very clever. He came quietly and peaceably with his religion. We were amused at his foolishness and allowed him to stay. Now he has won our brothers, and our clan can no longer act as one. He has *put a knife on the things that held us together* and *we have fallen apart.*[11]

Troubled by his people's failure to become part of his resistance, Okonkwo takes up the village's crusade himself and kills one of the district commissioner's messengers. Disappointed by the lack of support from his clan, he turns his anger and despair inwardly and commits suicide.

Okonkwo, throughout his entire life, wrestles with his *chi*, his *guardian spirit*, and this conflict contributes to his downfall. In the novel, Obierika, Okonkwo's friend, sums up both his anguish about his friend's suicide and the clan's anger with the colonial administrators. He eulogizes his friend in a trembling voice: "That man was one of the greatest men of Umuofia. You drove him to kill himself; and now he will be buried like a dog...."[12] The contrast Achebe makes here of Okonkwo being a great man of the old order but being reduced to a "dog" in the new one is significant. The tragic death of Okonkwo symbolizes, in short, the triumph of the white man's mission, which has turned a "great man" into a "dog."

The European colonial crusade was based on the contentious premise of "civilizing the native." Achebe ends his novel with the district commissioner's plan to write a book: "in the many years in which he had toiled to bring civilization to different parts of Africa, he had learned a number of things" and one of them "was never attend to such undignified details as cutting a hanged man from the tree. Such attention would give the natives a poor opinion of him."[13] The district commissioner provisionally chooses a title for his book, "The Pacification of the Primitive Tribes of the Lower Niger,"[14] an ironic reference to the white man's civilizing mission.

What Achebe cleverly presented in the novel was to cast doubt upon this mission and to challenge the narratives of its accompanying storytellers. Achebe presents a world in which Igbos lived in organized and self-regulating civil communities. Is this not what civilization is? Europeans disturbed that orderly rhythm, but life still went on. The district commissioner's plan to tell a story that would not give due weight to local details exemplifies the *selectivity* of the colonial narrative. Civilizing the native to open up markets and to expand trade was the colonial story. To the Africans, this story was one-sided: colonialism was based on Europe's self-interest, self-righteousness, and alleged superiority, and its precepts were enforced with violence, exploitation, and domination of colonies.

When asked about what motivated the writing of *Things Fall Apart*, Achebe replied:

> Well, it's a very difficult question to answer, really. Because I can't put my finger on any particular thing. In a very general way, I was aware that my story had not yet been told, had not yet found its way to print. At Umuahia, we were initiated into reading fiction. And we encountered a lot of fiction about Africa and Africans. By the time I got to the University, there

was even a book about Nigeria which was put in our syllabus in English, *Mr. Johnson* by Joyce Cary. In other words, the idea of me in books had become for me a problem. That somehow, my story was not being told. There was a gap which needed to be filled.[15]

Achebe's need to fill this hiatus and to present the insiders' view of African culture was strong. He had the urge to write a story about how the Igbo people evolved to who they are today and where they came from, and this duly became the major stimulus to his early creative writing.

On the creative origins of *Things Fall Apart*, Achebe has commented: "I wanted to write the story about a family through three generations, the father, the son, the grandson; and so this was exactly what I did, and at that point I was rising in broadcasting and I was given one year...actually less than one year to study at the BBC in London."[16] After his stint there, Achebe, having retrieved the manuscript of his first novel that he had originally sent to an English writer for review, was somehow convinced that the story, as written, had not accomplished what he wanted to say. Before submitting the revised manuscript to Heinemann, he decided that the story should concentrate on the first generation: "At that point, I had decided that it was not quite the way I wanted it. That I was going to take it back into separate episodes, instead of three generations in one story— to have one generation in each story, making three books."[17]

Chinua Achebe's second novel in this three-generation saga is *No Longer at Ease*, first published in 1960. The title is from T.S. Eliot's poem, "The Journey of the Magi," part of which reads:

> *We returned to our places, these Kingdoms,*
> *But no longer at ease here, in the old dispensation,*
> *With an alien people clutching their gods.*

I should be glad of another death.[18]

The protagonist in this novel is Obiajulu Okonkwo (shortened into Obi Okonkwo), grandson of the *Things Fall Apart* hero. The setting is urban Nigeria in the 1950s. Obi Okonkwo has returned from his university studies in England, where he read English, contrary to his people's expectation that he would read law and return to defend them. His university education cost the princely sum of eight hundred British pounds, which was sponsored by the Umuofia Progressive Union, a village mutual help organization.[19] Obi was Umuofia's first son to acquire European education and a European-grade civil service job. He was treated like a village hero under the changing values of his village, which increasingly no longer recognized greatness as being defined through acquiring many *ozo* titles, barns, and children but rather stressed Christianity and Western education.

Returning from his studies, Obi is filled with youthful idealism, and he embarks on the ambitious path of reforming the Nigerian civil service. Eventually, however, he is ethically compromised. He has also alienated his own people by falling in love with Clara, an *osu*, social outcast, whom the Umuofia people found unacceptable. Because of mounting financial pressure from his ethnic group and his family, and the alienation from his mother and from Clara, Obi Okonkwo feels trapped—"no longer at ease in his own society." His idealism is lost, and he accepts the bribes offered to him. Mr. Green, a liberal colonial expatriate and Obi's boss, who often explained away the African's weaknesses with such dubious reasons as bad climate and tropical diseases, never understands the psychological crisis that ensnares Obi Okonkwo. Green does not realize that Obi is uncomfortable with the traditional Igbo world, and that he feels insecure because of his modern Western education. When Obi yields to economic pressures and begins to accept bribes, Mr. Green views Obi's entrapment as proof that "the African is corrupt through and through."[20]

No Longer at Ease captures the conflicts of a society in transition. Achebe dramatizes the perversity of corruption as it becomes systemic and as decadence becomes rooted in Nigerian society. The corrupt ways of the city are juxtaposed with the hard life and work of the rural areas, but the lure of materialism corrupts both urban and rural Nigerians. This corruption is demonstrated in the Umuofia people's response when their native son, Obi, faces a prison sentence for bribery. The principle of the bribery is not condemned; rather they question the meagerness of the bribe he took. They proclaim that if a man wants to eat a toad, he "should look for a fat and juicy one."[21]

For his third novel, *Arrow of God (1964)*, Achebe borrowed the title from his friend Christopher Okigbo's celebrated poem, "Come Thunder." The lines, quoted earlier, read as follows:

> *Magic birds with the miracle of lightning flash on their feathers...*
> *The arrows of God tremble at the gates of light,*
> *The drums of curfew pander to a dance of death,*[22]

Arrow of God, which implies that human beings are instruments of some higher divine purpose, is an apt title for a novel about life in Igboland after the period when things fell apart. Historically, the novel is a continuation of Achebe's first book but it also explores the idea of accommodation between the old and the new religions.

Arrow of God is set in the 1920s, during the period when the policies of the British colonial government changed from "pacification" to "indirect rule" and then to "direct rule" over Nigeria. Chronologically, it is the middle work in the trilogy.

The protagonist of the novel is Ezeulu, chief priest of the high god Ulu, the totemic snake cult, which protects six villages in the region of Umuaro: Umuachala, Umunneora, Umuagu, Umuezeani, Umuogwugwu, and Umuisiuzo. Until the villages united as Umuaro under the protection of the god Ulu, they worshipped various deities and suffered deadly attacks by warriors from Abam. Since uniting under Ulu, they have become invincible.[23]

In the novel, Ezeulu is committed to tradition, but decides to send his son Oduche to mission school to learn about the ways and secrets of the white man. As Ezeulu explains:

I want one of my sons to join these people and be my eye there. If there is nothing in it you will come back. But if there is something there you will bring home my share. The world is like a mask dancing. If you want to see it well you do not stand in one place. My spirit tells me that those who do not befriend the white man today will be saying had we known tomorrow.[24]

As chief priest of Ulu, Ezeulu's decision to send his son to mission school is seen as betrayal by the leaders of his clan. Moreover, when Ezeulu's son returns, he does not bring magical powers and strength; he brings decay and destruction. The attendant risks in Ezeulu's choice are captured in a proverbial passage in the novel: "The man who brings ant-ridden faggots into his hut should expect the visits of lizards. But if Ezeulu is now telling us that he is tired of the white man's friendship our advice to him should be: You tied the knot, you should also know how to undo it. You passed the shit that is smelling; you should carry it away."[25]

Achebe dramatizes Africa's internal tensions in this novel. Sending a son to mission school is an unexpected move for a high priest; in doing so, Ezeulu intends to hedge his bets against all political odds, be they related to tradition or to modernity. The dilemma of Ezeulu's decision is amplified when his Western-educated son, in his zeal as a convert, is caught trying to kill the sacred python, the symbol of clan unity. This heretical act destroys the center of Umuaro's way of life.[26] Ezeulu accepts responsibility for this abomination, but also blames his clan for initially failing to oppose the coming of the white man. In the story, Ezeulu also comes into conflict with the British district commissioner, Captain T.K. Winterbottom, by refusing to accept an official appointment as chief of Umuaro. Out of misunderstanding, Ezeulu is imprisoned for thirty-two days. After his release, Ezeulu sees himself as *"an arrow in the bow of his god," "the whip with which Ulu flogs Umuaro,"* the instrument by which his god intends to punish his people. Ezeulu, therefore, refuses to perform the required rituals before the new yams can be harvested. His refusal causes a crisis that results in the ruin of Ezeulu, his priesthood, and his traditional religion.[27] In *Arrow of God*, Achebe suggests again that African traditions were unable to withstand the force of the colonial encounter.

Arrow of God has been more controversial than other Achebe novels. Critics like Nigeria's Charles Nnolim have accused Achebe of borrowing heavily from *"The History of Umuchu,"* a pamphlet by his relative Simon Alagbogu Nnolim.[28] Charles Nnolim cited similarities in text and references. Achebe denies any significant indebtedness, but admits being influenced by S.A. Nnolim. C. Lynn Innes, a renowned Chinua Achebe scholar, has come to Achebe's defence by arguing that Charles Nnolim's "claims that it is the only source and that Achebe must have had [S.A.] Nnolim's pamphlet before him as he wrote are unconvincing and irresponsible."[29] Innes agrees that S.A. Nnolim's influence is clear, in that Achebe "met Simon Alagbogu Nnolim in 1957 and interviewed him in Umuchu, where he spent three days with the Eastern Nigerian Broadcasting Company."[30] Charles Nnolim's claims that "Achebe did not merely take the story of the High Priest and blow life into it, as Shakespeare did when borrowing material for *Julius Caesar* from Plutarch's *Lives of the Noble Grecians and the Romans* but went further" are, in Innes's view, grossly exaggerated. Innes compared Charles Nnolim to one of Chinua Achebe's fictional characters, Ofoedu, who "opened his mouth to let out his words alive without giving them as much as a bite with his teeth."[31]

Some critics regard *Arrow of God* as the great Igbo novel. The British critic Molly M. Mahood described it as Achebe's "richest book to date."[32] For Achebe himself, *Arrow of God* has "a peculiar quality" that makes it the book he is "most likely to be caught sitting down to read again."[33] As much as Chinua believes that choosing a favorite among his novels was "fully comparable to asking a man to list his children in the order in which he loves them," particularly given "the peculiar attractiveness of each child,"[34] nonetheless *Arrow of God* occupies a special place in the writer's total output.

Chinua's fourth novel, *A Man of the People (1966)*, is a veritable saga on political corruption in postcolonial Africa. Also set in Nigeria, one of the novel's main characters is a handsome chief, the Honorable M.A. Nanga, M.P. and minister of culture. The reader learns that Nanga was originally from the village of Anata and was the "most approachable politician in the country."[35] The other important character is Mr. Odili Samalu, the idealistic young teacher who narrates the novel. Chief Nanga and Mr. Samalu, in representing opposite poles of the political spectrum, frame the problem of political morality within the novel. Odili, influenced by his Western education, has a detached approach to local politics, shunning corruption and avoiding traditional allegiances that he describes as "primitive loyalties." Nanga, on the other hand, is a pragmatist who, by hook or by crook, exploits "primitive loyalties" to grab his share of the "national cake" and to enhance his material comfort. Though he maintains close touch with the people, he lacks any social conscience. His many admirers, including Odili's father, respond to any criticism leveled against Nanga by asking whether "a sensible man would spit out the juicy morsel that good fortune placed in his mouth."[36]

Ironically, Chief Nanga was once Odili's teacher. Odili cannot understand how a man as corrupt as Nanga, who had pushed the nation down the slippery "slopes of inflation," can be so popular, particularly among the ordinary folk, the most obvious victims of his policies.

In the novel, before the general election that the People's Organization Party (POP) expects to win, international coffee prices fall. The finance minister, a world-class economist with a Ph.D. in public finance, holds a cabinet majority, and recommends cuts in subsidies to coffee farmers, who are the bulwark of the government's political support. The prime minister, however, backed by Nanga, ignores the political cost; instead he orders the National Bank to print more money, which results in inflation. The prime minister then embarks on a "witchhunt" and dismisses all the European-educated ministers, including the finance minister, whom he labelled the "Miscreant Gang" because of their nefarious plot to overthrow his government.[37] Nanga is delighted by the prime minister's actions, because he had his eye on one of the vacancies.

Throughout the story, Nanga lives the high life. Using the "carrot and whip" approach, he masterfully maintains control of his constituency. Even Odili's village of Urua comes under Nanga's dispensation. He wins the villagers' support by giving them "a slice of the national cake." He provides public assets to particular villages—tarred roads, for example, with an eye to winning their votes. At times he uses the "whip" and withholds public assets—water pipes in the case of the village of Urua—until the village elders reassure him of their support.

In one episode, a character named Josiah is a telling parable about the degree of political corruption and callousness depicted in the story. Josiah tries to trick a blind man by getting him drunk on palmwine and substituting his walking stick with a stand-in so that he can take the stick to use for juju. This attempted slight of hand illustrates how politicians, like Nanga, "have taken away enough for the owner to notice."[38]

A turning point in the story occurs when Nanga outmaneuvers Odili and sleeps with his girlfriend, Elsie, an acquisitive city girl who is not inhibited about having a one-night stand. Odili turns against Nanga to revenge this deed and to assuage his damaged pride. He asserts his manhood by courting Edna, Nanga's future wife. He also joins an old friend, Max, in his newly created political party, the Common People's Convention (CPC), to contest Nanga's seat. The CPC is supported by the young overseas-educated elite and is financed by the Soviet bloc. In his dual-revenge campaign, Odili draws closer to Edna and campaigns vigorously against Nanga's re-election. Corruption and violence, however, rock the campaign. Nanga uses intimidation, bribery, and any other illicit weapons at his disposal to be re-elected. The situation degenerates. Max is killed and becomes a hero of the revolution. Gangs of political hooligans and thugs riot in the streets after the elections. The ambitious military, frustrated by the corruption and the anarchy, stages a *coup d'état*. Nanga is arrested as he attempts to escape the country by canoe, disguised as a fisherman.[39]

A Man of the People documents a particular mood of political development in Africa, particularly in Nigeria during the politically charged events of late 1964, which gave rise to the army's venture into the national political arena. Achebe caustically captures the gullibility of ordinary people and the cynicism of leaders who abuse political power, which ultimately result in broad-based corruption; he shows the indifference, greed, and complacency of the elite- all this setting the stage for the army's intrusion into national public life on the pretext of "cleaning house."

Achebe's fifth novel *Anthills of the Savannah (1987)* is about the military and its role in a contemporary West African state. It could be argued that *Anthills of the Savannah* picks up twenty years after *A Man of the People*, after the *coup d'état*. The story begins and ends with a coup, allegorically implying that when African states lack a functioning social contract with stable political and moral values and rules, the army, despite its imperfections, is forced to step in as a sad corrective to political ineptitude.

Anthills of the Savannah is set in the fictional West African state of Kangan. The novel is peopled by four main characters: Sam, the Sandhurst-trained military head of state; Christopher Oriko, Sam's childhood friend and a commissioner of information in Sam's cabinet; Ikem Osodi, a poet and the editor of the government-owned *National Gazette,* also Sam's friend; and Beatrice Okoh, Chris's lover, strong and pretty, university educated in London, and a top government official.

The novel is organized around a sequence of testimonies by the main characters as witnesses to the troubles of military rule in Kangan state. Since the novel is set in the politically and economically complex period of the 1980s, Achebe, not satisfied with the one person narrative, employs a cross-section of perspectives. In the book, two years after the military coup that brought Sam, the young army officer, to the throne- the "golden stool" of Kangan- Sam has already assumed such elegant titles as "His Excellency." It is not "excellency" that Sam exudes, however, but an arbitrary tyranny that he visits with brute force on even his oldest and most loyal friends. Achebe depicts this tyrant's unpredictability with characteristic humor, "Days are good or bad...according to how His Excellency gets out of bed in the morning."[40]

Early chapters of the novel contain several witnesses to the dictator's pathology. Even Chris Oriko, Sam's old friend, discovers that his days are numbered, and Ikem Osodi, another friend, discovers that his tough criticism of the government is in vain against a regime where freedoms are suppressed and fear rules. Both Chris and Ikem become increasingly unhappy with Sam's intrusive authoritarianism. The steady erosion in their power makes them identify more with the plight of ordinary people in such perilous times. It also targets them for political reprisals, and both die resisting the brutal abuse of power.

In the end, another coup eliminates Sam.[41] Interestingly enough, it is Beatrice and the strong group of women she has nurtured who point the way out of the hopelessness and mindless violence of masculine power. In *Anthills of the Savannah,*

Achebe— who has sometimes been accused of sexism in his novels— entrusts the women with the tasks of national renewal and the return to political sanity.

All five of Chinua Achebe's novels reveal a continuing engagement with the evolution of Nigerian society and a deep concern about its unstable politics. Although the setting of *Things Fall Apart*, predates the British colonial construct called Nigeria, the subsequent novels engage the unwieldy polity that is Nigeria, and they point to beacons that might redeem its malaise. In his most recent novel, *Anthills of the Savannah*, Achebe questions traditional masculine authority, especially as manifested in the military, that has so dismally failed in Nigeria. The future, Achebe suggests, may lie in the more temperate and nurturing qualities of Nigeria's women.

NOTES

1. Quoted in Achebe's *A Man of the People* (1989), Anchor book blurb.
2. Quoted in Achebe's *No Longer at Ease* (1969), Fawcett Premier book blurb.
3. Quoted in Achebe's *A Man of the People* (1967), Anchor book blurb.
4. Quoted in Achebe's *Arrow of God* (1989), Anchor book blurb.
5. Ibid.
6. Quoted in Fawcett Premier book blurb, op. cit.
7. William Butler Yeats, "The Second Coming" in Richard J. Finneran, ed., *The Yeats Reader* (New York: Scribner Poetry, 1997), p. 68.
8. Achebe, *Things Fall Apart* (New York: Anchor Books, 1994), p. 13.
9. Ibid., p. 8.
10. Ibid., p. 176.
11. Ibid.
12. Ibid., p. 208.
13. Ibid.
14. Ibid., p. 209.
15. Authors' interview with Chinua Achebe, March 1995.
16. Ibid.
17. Ibid.
18. T.S. Eliot, "The Journey of the Magi," in *The Wasteland and Other Poems* (New York, Harcourt Brace Jovanovich, 1962), p. 70.
19. Chinua Achebe, *No Longer at Ease* (New York:Anchor Books, 1994), p. 8.
20. Ibid., p. 3.
21. Ibid., p. 7.
22. Okigbo, *Labyrinth*, p. 66.
23. Achebe, *Arrow of God*, pp. 14-15; p. 70.
24. Ibid., p. 46.
25. Ibid., p. 144.
26. Ibid., p. 191.
27. Ibid., p. 208-230
28. Charles Nnolim, "A Source for Arrow of God," in C.L. Innes and Bernth Lindfors, eds., *Critical Perspectives on Chinua Achebe* (Washington: Three Continents Press, 1978), pp. 219-243.
29. C.L. Innes, "A Source for Arrow of God: A Response," in C.L. Innes and Bernth Lindfors, eds., *Critical Perspectives*, op. cit., p. 245.
30. Ibid.
31. Ibid., p. 244.

32. M. M. Mahood, "Idols of the Den: Achebe's Arrow of God," in Innes and Lindfors, pp. 181.
33. Achebe, Preface to Edition of *Arrow of God* (1989)
34. Ibid.
35. Achebe, *Man of the People*, p. 1.
36. Ibid., pp. 2-3.
37. Ibid., p. 5.
38. Ibid., p. 86.
39. Ibid., pp. 145-148.
40. Achebe, *Anthills of the Savannah*, p. 2.
41. Ibid., p. 202.

CHAPTER 13

The Eagle and the Hunters: Achebe and Controversy

Although Achebe never shies away from controversy, he picks his fights carefully. And when he fights, he is an invincible warrior. In 1983, a critical point in Nigeria's history, he published a tiny book, which he called a "little pamphlet," titled *The Trouble with Nigeria*. The fact that the book was published by a local Nigerian publisher, Fourth Dimensions Publishing Company, indicated that Achebe's immediate choice of audience was Nigerians. The book startled Nigerian readers by its truths, expressed in Achebe's vintage bluntness:

> The trouble with Nigeria is simply and squarely a failure of leadership. There is nothing basically wrong with the Nigerian character. There is nothing wrong with the Nigerian land or climate or water or air or anything else. The Nigerian problem is the unwillingness or inability of its leaders to rise to the responsibility, to the challenge of personal example which are the hallmarks of true leadership.[1]

With the problem clearly identified, Achebe gave examples of how a Nigerian military leader, Murtala Muhammed, a northerner who led by good example, was within a short period able to restore order and discipline to public life in Nigeria. Achebe went on to add that "the character of one man could establish that quantum change in a people's behavior was nothing less than miraculous. But it shows that social miracles can happen."[2]

In the book Achebe harshly discusses Nigerian tribalism, false images of itself, leadership, patriotism, social injustice, and the cult of mediocrity, indiscipline, corruption, the "Igbo problem," and the example of the leader Malam Aminu Kano, another northerner, whose words and actions exemplified the high purpose of politics. He derided two early Nigerian leaders: Dr. Nnamdi Azikiwe (or Zik), an Igbo and Nigeria's first president, and Chief Obafemi Awolowo, a Yoruba and former premier of western Nigeria. He criticized Zik for his "consistent ambivalence to his ethnic homeland [Igboland]" and for "abandonment of Igbo people in their darkest hour."[3] He also criticized Awolowo, whom Yorubas idolized almost as a saint, for his narrow Ijebu-Yoruba nationalism and his anti-Igbo politics, and for seeking and using his talent to serve a narrow purpose.[4] Achebe's harsh criticism was not always well received, especially among some Yorubas, who interpret his anti-Awolowo views as anti-Yoruba.

Some of the Yoruba sentiments against Achebe arose when Wole Soyinka won the 1986 Nobel Prize for Literature. Some Yoruba interpreted the prize not as a continental or national celebration, but as an ethnic celebration. The prize, for good reasons, was greeted with much pride and excitement for Soyinka all over Africa, the black diaspora, and certainly in Nigeria. It was recognition that modern African literature had come of age. The Nobel citation praises Soyinka, "who in a wide cultural perspective and with poetic overtones fashions the drama of existence."[5] The Swedish Academy's praised Soyinka's work for its "moral stature" and Soyinka himself for "possessing a prolific store of words and expressions which he exploits to the full in witty dialogue, in satire and grotesquery, in quiet poetry and essays of sparkling vitality."[6] The academy made special mention of Soyinka's plays, *A Dance of the Forests* and *Death and the King's Horseman,* and commented: "A key figure in Soyinka, the god Ogun, also appears in the play. He is both creator and destroyer and, as Soyinka sees him, has traits that lead one's thought to the Dionysian, the Appolonian, and Promethean in European tradition."[7]

Although Soyinka's award dominated the headlines for weeks in Nigeria, there were grumbles beneath the excitement. One of the harshest critics was Chinweizu, a friend and protegé of Achebe. Chinweizu, who had become a notorious Soyinka critic in his book, *Towards the Decolonization of African Literature,* published an essay in 1985 (a year before Soyinka's Nobel Prize) in *The Guardian,* one of Nigeria's leading dailies, entitled, "That Nobel Prize Brouhaha." In that essay, Chinweizu had commented, reacting to a colleague's disappointment that the Newsweek 1985 speculation that an African writer would receive the Nobel Prize did not come true: "Somebody asked what I thought of the prize not having gone to Soyinka. Well, I was actually disappointed. In my view, the Nobel Prize and Soyinka's works deserve one another. It would be an excellent case of the undesirable honoring the unreadable."[8] Chinweizu was being unfairly partisan, for the Nobel Prize is desirable and many of Soyinka's works are readable. Chinweizu went on to argue about European intellectual arrogance and power play; that "a gaggle of Swedes, all by themselves, should pronounce on intellectual excellence for the diverse cultures of the whole wide world."[9] Chinweizu raised important questions but was not kind to Soyinka. To some of Chinweizu's critics, this unkindness to Soyinka was a reflection of his partisanship on behalf of his patron-saint, Chinua Achebe, who did not receive the prize.

At the Association of Nigerian Authors' meeting in Lagos in December 1986, Achebe remarked on the prize during his final address as president of the association at a time when major writers such as Soyinka and J.P. Clark were present:

> This is the year of Wole Soyinka's Nobel Prize. We rejoice with him on his magnificent achievement. A lot has already been said or written about it and no doubt more will be said. For me what matters is that after the *oriki* we should say to ourselves: One of us has proved that we can beat the white man at his own game. That is wonderful for us and for the white man. But now we must turn away and play our own game.[10]

Achebe's use of the term *"oriki"* was a reference to a traditional form of Yoruba poetry. Was he being provocative? Some people argued that Achebe was jealous that he did not receive the prize.[11] Achebe's subsequent remarks did not help matters. He noted, "The Nobel award for literature is a European prize and did not make any African the *asiwaju* (Yoruba chief) of Nigerian literature."[12] These and other occasional remarks on national issues directed against some Yoruba public figures disturbed those who wanted to see Achebe as a detribalized national hero.[13]

Some people argued that Achebe did not get the Nobel Prize because of his refusal to participate in the Second Conference of African Writers in 1986 in Stockholm, Sweden, the seat (alternating with Oslo, Norway) of the award. In a reply to their invitation, he said:

> I regret I cannot accept your generous invitation for the simple reason that I do not consider it appropriate for African writers to assemble in European capitals in 1986 to discuss the future of their literature. In my humble opinion, it smacks too much of those constitutional conferences arranged in Lon-

don and Paris for our pre-independence political leaders. Believe me, this is not an attempt to belittle the efforts and concern of your organization or indeed of the Swedish people who have repeatedly demonstrated their solidarity with African aspirations in many different ways. But I strongly believe that the time is overdue for Africans, especially African writers, to begin to take the initiative in deciding the things that belong to their peace.[14]

Achebe was not the only writer who declined the invitation; the Ghanaian Ayi Kwei Armah also did so. Several years prior to the conference, Achebe was featured in newspapers and magazines as a strong contender (together with Wole Soyinka and Senegal's Leopold Sedar Senghor) for the Nobel prize, and there was talk in the press that it was Africa's time to receive it. Was his principled stance to decline attendance of the Stockholm conference seen as an offensive bluff to the Nobel Committee and therefore required a public rebuff? One may never know. The fact is that he was not awarded the prize, even though he is one of those who most deserved it. Ironically, one rarely encounters anyone familiar with African literature who does not mention Achebe's *Things Fall Apart* as the only work of African literature they have read. The joke spreading around following Soyinka's award was that, people kept asking: "Who is the greatest Nigerian writer?" Answer: "Wole Soyinka." "Ah, and what was his greatest book?" Answer: "*Things Fall Apart.*"[15]

The Nobel Committee's oversight and the popularity of his books aside, Achebe takes positions when it comes to evaluating the record of Nigeria's leaders. In May 1987, Chief Obafemi Awolowo died. Mourning of his loss and celebration of his achievements dominated the Nigerian press. Even Biafra's former leader, Chief Chukwuemeka Odumegwu Ojukwu, joined in the eulogies, claiming, "Awolowo was the best president Nigeria never had."[16] Achebe, however, thought

Awolowo did not merit such a national honor. In a statement, not well received in some Yoruba quarters where Awolowo was revered, Achebe dissented from the prevailing public opinion. "Chief Obafemi Awolowo," he said, "was a great leader, in so far as he was both a Nigerian and a leader. But his contributions to Nigerian public affairs in the last years did not qualify him as a great national leader, rather he was a champion of a section of the geographical expression called Nigeria."[17] Achebe carefully and diplomatically crafted his words; for him Awolowo was a sectional nationalist.

In debates about the works of writers who denigrate Africa, Achebe is equally fierce in his criticism. In his lecture titled, "An Image of Africa: Racism in Conrad's *Heart of Darkness*," Achebe argued that the Polish-born, French-speaking, English sea captain and novelist, Joseph Conrad was "a thoroughgoing racist."[18] An American journalist called Achebe's remarks an "angry essay."[19] The journalist went on to add, "Mr. Achebe takes such Western writers as Conrad- and his readers- to task for seeing Africa only as a foil to Europe, darkness pitted against civilization. Many critics interpret the essay as saying, Don't read Conrad."[20] Achebe, however, hardly recommended book banning in his essay. Instead, he argued that Conrad was a storyteller who denied humanity to his African characters, who wrote eloquently to invigorate the myth of imperialism. For these reasons, he was a writer denigrating Africans in the service of empire.[21]

In a lecture delivered at W.E.B. Dubois Institute for Afro-American research at Harvard University titled "Today, the Balance of Stories" published in his most recent book of essays, *Home and Exile*, Achebe confronted still another apologist for empire, but this time someone who came from the periphery of the empire, the Oxford-educated Trinidadian writer and Nobel Laureate, Sir Vidiadhar Surajprasad Naipaul, widely known as V.S. Naipaul. For Achebe, Naipaul is a modern-day apprentice of Conrad, if not a worse replica. Naipaul's own ancestry is Indian, but his vocation has often led him to various troubled spots of the world, including India and Africa, about which he has written scathing, unsympathetic accounts. Achebe wrote, "The poverty in India, his ancestral home, filled him with disgust, and his reaction brought him into conflict with many Indians who were not necessarily defensive but still found his attitude too insensitive, arrogant and plain ignorant."[22]

Naipaul opens his novel *A Bend in the River*, set in Africa, with provocative words: "The world is what it is: men who are nothing, who allow themselves to become nothing, have no place in it."[23] Achebe called this "pontifical high writing. Where do you find these men he speaks about who are nothing? And what do you mean by nothing?"[24] Taking Naipaul's narrative and biased perspective to task, Achebe concluded that Naipaul's writing is not "merely troubling," it is "downright outrageous."[25] He argued that Naipaul's novel was modeled on Conrad's *Heart of Darkness*. Whereas Conrad gave us "an Africa of malignant mystery and incomprehensibility, Naipaul's method was to ridicule claims to any human achievement in Africa."[26]

Unrelenting and tough-minded in his argument, Achebe further noted:

> Naipaul's narrator, Salim, is an Indian shopkeeper whose forefathers had been brought by the British to work in their East African colonies in much the same way as Naipaul's people were taken to Trinidad. Salim's qualification for narrator of Naipaul's African story is slim. Although he had grown up in East Africa, he did not really know Africans; he had lived in a closed Indian community whose attitude was to look down on the Africans. Naipaul could have used this limitation to call the trustworthiness of Salim's narrative into question and, in that way, written a different kind of book. But he evidently had no such intention. He held Africans in deep contempt himself, and made no secret of it. Although

he was writing about Africa, he was not writing for Africans.[27]

Achebe did not believe Naipaul wrote only this way about Africans. As he noted, "About Asians, he wasn't much kinder."[28]

On April 9, 1980, as invited keynote speakers at the annual meeting of the United States-based African Literature Association at the University of Florida in Gainesville, Chinua Achebe met with the African-American writer James Baldwin for the first time. Their theme was to engage in a dialogue to define the "African" or "black aesthetic." Both writers had admired each other's works before they met and, before their public dialogue, they were sequestered together with long-time friends. When they got to the conference stage, they continued their conversation with warm regard for each other. Achebe opened the conversation with the following:

> When I met Jimmy Baldwin and it seems I have known him [for a long time], although we just met yesterday. When I read *Go Tell It On The Mountain* in 1958, I knew here was a brother. And so I immediately proceeded to the American Information Service in the city where I lived to borrow some more books by Baldwin. Unfortunately, there were no other books by Baldwin, or anybody like him, in that library. And so I asked, "How come there are no books by Baldwin in this library?" I must say in fairness to the people concerned, they were moved and that situation was changed. Well that was 1958. A lot has happened in that time. And when I met him yesterday I nearly said, "Mr. Baldwin, I presume."[29]

Baldwin also spoke sympathetically about this historical coming together:

> I'll even say of a somewhat unprecedented nature, my buddy whom I met yesterday, my brother whom I met yester-

130

day— who I have not seen in 400 years, it was never intended that we should meet.[30]

Further into the conversation, he added:

When I read *Things Fall Apart* ... which is about an Igbo tribe in Nigeria, a tribe I never saw, a system- to put it that way- or a society, the rules of which were a mystery to me, I recognized everybody in it. And that book was about my father. How we got over I don't know, we did![31]

After both speakers fraternal opening remarks, Achebe spoke of the African experiences that defined his aesthetics, while Baldwin spoke of his African-American experiences. Achebe said:

The topic of [an] African aesthetic is one ...I am very diffident about, because I didn't know if I could define aesthetic initially. And I am not sure, in fact, that we are operating on the same wave length.... But if by aesthetic we mean those qualities of excellence which culture discerns from its works of art, then I will accept it. We do have an aesthetic. We had it and we have it! Now...it's easier to say that than to tell you what it is.[32]

He then attempted to do so:

Now we can look at our aesthetic from our traditional culture. ...And I'd like to say...that in my understanding, aesthetic cannot be fixed, immutable. It has to change as the occasion demands because in our understanding, art is made by man for man, and therefore, according to the needs of man, his qualities of excellence. What he looks for in art will also change. So if somebody is thinking of aesthetics handed down like logs to Moses, that is not the kind of thing we are talking about. We are talking about what our ancestors considered important in the stories they told, in their proverbs, in their legends, and their myths: why they repeated certain things over and over again. This is very important. This is what I understand. ...I also understand that we are now in the twentieth century, and therefore we are not simply receivers of aesthetics...we are makers of aesthetics.[33]

Achebe then went on to single out aspects of African aesthetics—especially that art had a social purpose, because it belonged to people. Art was also political, and he argued that people who said "Do not put too much politics in your art" were not being honest. What those people meant was "don't upset the system."[34] He also argued that "art cannot be on the side of the oppressor. When Yevtushenko, the Russian poet, said that a poet cannot be a slave trader at the same time, he was absolutely right."[35] Achebe further noted, "There are many slave traders who would like to be poets; they are entitled to be poets: but please, one job at a time. If you look at our aesthetics you will find this, that art is in the service of man. Art was not created to dominate and destroy man. Art is made by man for his own comfort."[36]

Achebe further went on to highlight the holistic approach of his people's art, that everything mattered, including the newly arrived white man, and also that morality is central to art.

James Baldwin picked up Achebe's remarks and spoke with a directness and toughness of manner characteristic of his sharp intellect:

> I think when Chinua talks about aesthetic, beneath that word sleeps—think it—the word morality. And beneath that word we are confronted with the way we treat each other. That is the key to morality. Now I want to suggest a difficult proposition to my innocent countrymen. I want you to think about this. This is 1980. The century has 20 years to go. I will still be here I assure you because I am stubborn, - until the year 2000. But I was here at the beginning of the

century too....[37]

Unfortunately, time did not bear out James Baldwin's prophecy. He did not live to see the end of the millennium; but perhaps he did through the spirit of his works.

One of the low points of the Achebe/Baldwin encounter in Florida occurred when some white males interrupted, using racist slurs as Baldwin spoke. Baldwin was reminding the crowd:

> Do not forget it was not a thousand years ago that it was a crime to teach a slave to read or write. Do not forget either, in this country that calls itself a white country there are all the colors under heaven. To put it a little brutally—but as an old black lady said to me nearly thirty years ago in Alabama (and I'm quoting her), "White people don't hate black people. If they did we'd all be black."[38]

At that moment, some white males interfered with the microphone, which was followed by a thunderous laughter from the startled audience. A white male cried out, "You gonna have to cut it out Mr. Baldwin. We can't stand for this kind of going on."[39] The voice continued with more angry words.

It seemed as if their words stirred in Baldwin that stubborn spirit of a fearless freedom fighter. No longer patient, he spoke forcefully into the microphone:

> Mr. Baldwin is nevertheless going to finish his statement. And I will tell you now, whoever you are, that if you assassinate me in the next two minutes, I'm telling you this: it no longer matters what you think. The doctrine of white supremacy on which the Western world is based has had its hour— has had its day! It's over![40]

The excited audience supported Baldwin with shouts of "Right on!" and more applause. As Baldwin took his seat, the mod-

erator, Bowling Green University's professor of ethnic studies, Ernest Champion (a former Sri Lankan national), rose to
the podium and commanded the audience to silence. "It is
quite obvious," he remarked, "that we are in the eye of the
hurricane. But having this dialogue is quite important so all
of us in this room will take it seriously."[41] This said, the ground
rules for submitting questions were agreed upon, and the conversation continued, including even a question to Achebe about
his views of Wole Soyinka's clever statement on Negritude,
that a "tiger cannot proclaim its tigritude." The concept of
Negritude was initiated in 1934 in Paris by Francophone black
intellectuals such as Leopold Sedar Senghor of Senegal, Aime
Cesaire of Martinique, and Leon Gotran Damas of French
Guiana, who created a black arts movement in celebration of
the glories of African culture and the human-centered sim-
plicity of African civilizations, and in response to France's
cultural policy of *assimilation* in its overseas colonies. The
Negritude writers have made considerable contribution to the
world's great poetry.

Not entirely sold on the anti-Negritude bandwagon,
Achebe replied:

> Yes, we heard that. It is a very clever quip.... What you have
> not heard is the profound response which Senghor made.
> He said, "A tiger does not talk." Now I'm quoting myself
> because I used this information not so long ago. "The Ne-
> gro talks and talking is part of his humanity. So don't com-
> pare me with a tiger. A tiger has not been oppressed in the
> forest; I have." So it is clever in a superficial way. Which is
> not to say that you cannot quarrel with the founders of
> Negritude and what they are doing today. That's another
> story. But don't say that because somebody is mismanaging
> certain affairs today that the poetry he wrote twenty years
> ago is bad.[42]

For Achebe, Negritude had received a "bad rap" in English

speaking Africa because Soyinka, as a literary hero, challenged it as self-glorification by Frenchified black intellectuals. Many critics, however, lost the essence of what Negritude was trying to do, restore black dignity through celebration of the achievements of black civilizations. In short, Negritude broke the monologue that Europe had with Africa. By having eloquent Africans speaking for themselves, Negritude forced a dialogue. Europe was forced to take notice; to switch roles, and to listen.

On June 17, 1998, Achebe presented the Presidential Fellow Lecture, "Africa Is People," a World Bank event hosted by the bank's president, James D. Wolfensohn. The address was part of a distinguished lecture series that had featured speakers such as the minister-president of Saxony, Germany, Kurt Biedenkopf; Nobel Laureate Amartya Sen; and Ema Rothschild. The auditorium was packed beyond capacity so much so that President Wolfensohn expressed amazement in his opening remarks. "With this," he quipped to Achebe, "maybe you should be president."[43] Achebe began his lecture recounting an invitation he had accepted at a meeting of the Organization for Economic Cooperation and Development (OECD) in Paris, where he was the odd man out, a novelist among bankers, economists and other people of finance. Puzzled by the reason for his invitation to the meeting, he listened to them spin theories about why there was so much poverty in the developing world which, according to Achebe, they explained as due to all kinds of indiscipline. Structural adjustment, a process of strict policy reform backed by conditionalities—included freeing prices, cutting public spending through removing food and fuel subsidies, privatizing public assets, and devaluing national currencies—was the solution, what Achebe referred to as the "magic bullet of the 1980s."[44] Achebe criticized the harmful effects of some of these proposals on the poor, and criticized international bankers for their myopia and for their empty promises that "shock treatment" would work and that poor people simply needed patience. As Achebe listened at the OECD meeting, he realized that these finance people were engaged in a "fiction workshop."[45]

With the skillful effrontery of a writer who chooses his causes carefully, Achebe argued before the OECD gathering:

> Here you are spinning your fine theories to be tried out in your imaginary laboratories. You are developing new drugs and feeding them to a bunch of laboratory guinea pigs and hoping for the best. I have news for you. Africa is not fiction. Africa is people. Have you thought of that? You are brilliant people, world experts. You may even have the very best intentions. But have you thought, really thought of Africa as people?[46]

He went on to give examples of the typical flesh-and-blood man in his home country of Nigeria. The man had a wife and children, and found his miserable income halved under structural adjustment. Achebe's message of the harmful effects of international experimental finance policies on the poor was a direct plea to "experts" at the World Bank. To use his own metaphors, he had released his "conscience cat" among the "naughty pigeons" of world financiers.[47]

Continuing his speech at the World Bank, Achebe questioned the mythology of imperialism as exemplified in the words and actions of Western icons like Albert Schweitzer and Joseph Conrad. He questioned their ideologies, which had created a world whose language was brainwashing and whose agents built an oppressive architecture. He quoted from the essay "Fifth Avenue, Uptown" by his African American friend, James Baldwin, where the author exhorts black people to challenge the world imperialism had built:

> Negroes want to be treated like men: a perfectly straight

136

forward statement containing seven words. People who have mastered Kant, Hegel, Shakespeare, Marx, Freud and the Bible find this statement impenetrable.[48]

In view of the oppressive relations of the past, Achebe went on to plea that captains of global finance, donors and lenders, should *"do the right thing."* They should stop supporting corrupt African leaders. They should return the vast amount of Africa's stolen wealth in their vaults that continues to enrich their economies. They should cancel the debts owed by the world's poorest nations, especially in Africa. Achebe quoted Wolfensohn's statistic: "You will be staggered to know, as I was, that 37 percent of African private wealth is held outside Africa, whereas for Asia the share is 3 percent and for Latin America it is 17 percent."[49]

In his final plea, Achebe added:

It would be a great pity if the world were to sit back in the face of this tragedy and do nothing, merely to preserve codes of banking etiquette and confidentiality formulated for quite other times. The world woke up too late to the inadequacy of these codes in the matter of the Nazi Holocaust gold. We have now been warned. The cooperation of the world's banks led by the World Bank Group in eliminating the great scourge will give so many poor countries the first real opportunity to begin afresh and take responsibility for their development and progress, and it will discourage future marauders of nations. It will also clear the banks of the charge of receiving stolen property and even more severe indictments.[50]

With these words, Achebe received a standing ovation. His plea, as controversial as it may have seemed, was quite consistent with the new philosophy, championed by World Bank President Wolfensohn, of encouraging world financiers to do the right thing to stamp out corruption and to help the world's poor.

Political economy concerns aside, on the question of language, Achebe has not been silent. Whereas some African writers like the Kenyan Ngugi wa Thiong'o have advocated a return to African languages as the primary medium of literary expression, Achebe is not entirely comfortable with this idea. He has chosen to write mainly in English, which some critics say is the "language of imperialism." Achebe believes African writers should be free to write in whatever language they feel comfortable and should not be inhibited in their choice of language in the interest of political correctness. As an advocate for the use of English, Achebe has argued, "What would you put in its place? ...Africa has some 200-odd languages. The fact is, we require English to communicate with each other."[51]

On the issue of his native Igbo language, Achebe disagrees with the much locally praised value of "Union Igbo"— the standardized Igbo into which the Igbo Bible was translated. The Igbo Bible was translated in 1913 by an English missionary named Archdeacon T.J. Dennis, who sat at a table with a team of Igbo speakers from the four "leading" Igbo dialects (Onitsha, Bonny, Arochukwu, and Ugwana) and chose the "right" word, which was compiled as the authoritative standard text in Igboland. According to legend, Dennis was killed by enemy action during the First World War, and the box containing the Dennis translation of the Bible was miraculously washed ashore and retrieved by fishermen. Although convinced of the practical value of a single Igbo Bible, Achebe questioned the arbitrariness of the choice of four leading Igbo dialects and asked himself, "Leading in what?"[52] What about the other Igbo dialects? Achebe saw Union Igbo as ultimately harmful; it inhibited creativity in the Igbo dialects because it was not related to living speech; furthermore, Union Igbo lacked color, dramatic intensity, and poetry. "It seems afraid to act or rather too heavy and clumsy and self-conscious."[53] Achebe illustrated his argument with a "translation atrocity in Luke 2:52": "And Jesus increased in *wisdom* and *stature*," which is rendered as *Jisus we naga n'iru n'amam-ike na ogologo*; the atrocity being contained in *ogologo* which does not mean *stature* but *length*."[54]

Conscious of the strong link between literary language and living speech, Achebe is not afraid to plunge into controversy even in his immediate homeland. He argued:

> The point...is that notwitstanding Dennis' optimism and scholarship, or the magnitude of his labours, and nothwithstanding even the divine intervention to which legend ascribes the recovery of his manuscript, the ultimate result of his task has been more disastrous to the emergence of creative Igbo language and literature than any other single factor.[55]

In the evolution of European standard languages, there was a slow, organic development. Achebe argued, "The so-called Queen's English was not chosen by surveyors but by the dynamic laws of natural selection."[56] Achebe feared that "unless Igbo is able to create imaginative literature it will steadily go into eclipse."[57] So he recommended the need to free Igbo writers to write in whatever dialect they know and speak and not be inhibited by Union Igbo.

On the questions of Europe's civilizing mission in Africa and of whether he sees Europeans who came to Igboland as cruel villains, Chinua says that he did not see Europeans as mere villains in the colonial enterprise.

> I think they were very ignorant. And that's very bad, you know, when you are trying to civilize other people. But you don't really need to be blackhearted to do all kinds of wrong things. Those who have the best intentions sometimes commit the worst crimes. I think it's *not my business to present villains without any redeeming features*. This would be untrue. I think

what's more likely to be true is somebody coming with the best of intentions, *really believing that there is nothing here,* and that he is bringing civilization. *He's wrong, of course.* He's completely *wrong and misguided.* But that's the man that interests me because he has *potentialities for doing great harm.*[58]

Chinua Achebe's life as a writer has been deeply steeped in controversy. Whether in his native Igboland, in Nigeria, or in the wider world, Achebe has never stood on neutral ground. As a writer with a cause, he has attempted to take balanced positions, particularly in support of the rights of the dispossessed, articulating them lucidly inspite of any potential controversy. As he has said:

One big message of the many that I try to put across, is that Africa was not a vacuum before the coming of Europe, that culture was not unknown in Africa, that culture was not brought to Africa by the white world. .. People are expecting from literature serious comment on their lives. They are not expecting frivolity. They are expecting literature to say something important to help them in their struggle with life.... So it is a serious matter.[59]

Achebe's creative and critical writings have indeed been serious art, recreating with energy and skill individual and collective struggles in contemporary African life.

NOTES

.1 Chinua Achebe, *The Trouble With Nigeria* (Enugu, Nigeria: Fourth Dimension Publishing Co. Ltd., 1983), p. 1.

2. Ibid.

3. Ibid., p. 56.

4. Ibid., p. 64.

5. 1986 Nobel Prize Citation in literature, Swedish Academy; reproduced in Henry Louis Gates, Jr., ed., "Introduction," Wole Soyinka Issue, Part 1, *Black American Literature Forum*, 22, 3 (Fall 1988), p. 424.

6. Press Release (October 1986), The Nobel Prize in literature 1986- Wole Soyinka, Swedish Academy, *Black American Literature Forum*, 22,3 (Fall 1988), p. 426.

7. Ibid., p. 425.

8. Bernth Lindfors, "Beating the White Man at His Own Game," Ibid., p. 477.

9. Ibid.

10. Ibid., p. 487.

11. Awogbemila, "Master Craftsman," p. 17.

12. Ibid.

13. Ibid.

14. Ezenwa-Ohaeto, *Chinua Achebe*, pp. 241-242.

15. Charles Trueheart, "Chinua Achebe and the Politics of Art: The Novelist's Tales from a World Turned Upside Down," *Washington Post*, Tuesday, February 16,1988, p. D4.

16. Ezenwa-Ohaeto, *Chinua Achebe*, p. 251.

17. Ibid.

18. Karen J. Winkler, "An African Writer at a Crossroads," *The Chronicle of Higher Education*, 1/12 (1994), p. A9.

19. Ibid.

20. Ibid.

21. Awogbemila, "Master Craftsman," p. 23.

22. Achebe, *Home and Exile*, p. 86.

23. Ibid.

24. Ibid., pp. 86-87.

25. Ibid., p. 87.

26. Ibid., p. 88.

27. Ibid.

28. Ibid., p. 89.

29. Dorothy Randall Tsuruta, "In Dialogue to Define Aesthetics: James Baldwin and Chinua Achebe," *The Black Scholar*, 12, 2 (March/April 1981),

p. 73.
30. Ibid.
31. Ibid.
32. Ibid., p. 74.
33. Ibid.
34. Ibid., pp. 74-75.
35. Ibid., p. 75.
36. Ibid.
37. Ibid.
38. Ibid., p. 76.
39. Ibid.
40. Ibid.
41. Ibid.
42. Ibid., p. 78.
43. Authors' witness.
44. Chinua Achebe, *Africa Is People* (Washington, D.C.: The World Bank, 1998), p. 3.
45. Ibid., p. 4.
46. Ibid.
47. Ibid.
48. Ibid., p. 5.
49. Ibid., p. 8.
50. Ibid.
51. Winkler, "An African Writer," p. A9.
52. Chinua Achebe, "The Bane of Union: An Appraisal of the Consequences of Union Igbo for Igbo Language and Literature," ANA Magazine, 1(1979), p. 35.
53. Ibid., p. 38.
54. Ibid., p. 36.
55. Ibid., p. 34.
56. Ibid., p.38.
57. Ibid.
58. Bernth Lindfors et al., "Interview with Chinua Achebe," in *Conversations with Chinua Achebe* (Jackson: University of Mississippi, 1997), p. 30.
59. Ibid., p. 29.

CHAPTER 14

Eagle on Iroko:
Birthday
Celebration, Tragedy, and Hope

On February 11, 1990, Chinua Achebe's colleagues at the University of Nigeria, Nsukka, where he was a professor and chairman emeritus of the English department, organized an international conference, *"Eagle on Iroko: Chinua at 60"* to celebrate his birthday and to appraise his contributions to African and world literature and his many achievements as a broadcaster and active participant in Nigerian public life. The *iroko* is the tallest tree in Igboland, and the eagle is the king of birds in Igbo folklore. *"Eagle on Iroko"* meant the eagle had flown to the peak beyond the hunter's reach, suggesting Achebe's literary achievements have risen beyond the envy of detractors.

The conference began the same day when Nelson Mandela was freed from prison in South Africa, and the day was declared a national holiday.[1] Several admirers, i.e., academics, ambassadors, diplomatic representatives, journalists, writers, and even politicians came from all over the world to participate in the deliberations and festivities, which included presentations of scholarly papers, traditional dramas, dancing and banquets. Achebe's writing colleague, Wole Soyinka, sent him a white ram. The distinguished Nigerian critic, Emmanuel Obiechina, summoned the spirit of the celebration, saying, "I will call my tribute to Professor Chinua Achebe 'In Praise of THE TEACHER' because I regard Achebe as quintessentially a teacher." He went on to discuss Achebe's contributions to world literature and his relevance to Nigeria, to Africa, and to the World. To illustrate the relevance of Achebe's works, he noted, "Find any group of educated Nigerians in a street corner arguing irrepressibly as only Nigerians know how....and Chinua Achebe is bound to be introduced from time to time to set off an idea or support a point of view. Among Nigerians, appropriate quotations from Chinua Achebe are the palm-oil with which conversations are eaten."[2] Numerous doctoral theses have been written on Achebe's works. Obiechina further invoked the respect with which the teacher, *Onyenkuzi* (the person who straightened things out), was held in traditional Igbo society; *Onyenkuzi* is the synonym of *Onyengosi* (the revealer, the exposer). Thus, to Obiechina, *onyenkuzi's* double meaning was apt for Achebe, showing he was "a person who enlightens, who brings light to bear upon, who ... puts people on the path of knowing...."[3]

Several international writers, for example, the Somalian writer, Nuruddin Farah, and the American writer Joseph Bruchac, also heaped praises on Achebe's accomplishments. Perhaps the commentary in Nigeria's *Daily Times* by Godini G. Darah sums it up best:

> Those who still insist that prophets are not recognized in their countries should have been at Nsukka. Here were gathered people from all the continents of the earth to pay hom-

age to one of the most eloquent interpreters of their experiences: Chinua Achebe.[4]

These testimonies to Achebe's contributions were not surprising; he is the recipient of numerous international honors and awards, including twenty-five honorary doctorates from world-renowned universities, including Harvard University. In 1993, *The Times* of London even named Chinua as "one of the 1,000 'Makers of the 20th Century.'"[5]

Following the Nsukka festivities, Chinua planned to spend a semester at Stanford University, in California, as a visiting professor. Along with his son, Ikechukwu, he rented a car to take them from Enugu to Lagos. At Awka, on the divided highway linking Enugu and Onitsha, Achebe was in a terrible car accident. He sustained head lacerations, broken ribs, and spinal injuries which were serious enough to paralyze him from the waist down. Luckily, his son and the driver escaped with minor injuries. It was reported that the axle broke while the taxi was moving, and that Achebe and the vehicle were thrown in mid-air, with the sommersaulting automobile literally crashing with fearsome force on him.[6] Fortunately, at the site of the accident, a man named Okafor, a native of Awka, the birthplace of Achebe's mother, came to his rescue.[7] A local doctor administered emergency aid, and Achebe was later flown from Enugu to Paddocks Hospital in Buckinghamshire, England, where, over a period of several months, he underwent treatment and painful rehabilitation to straighten his spine.[8] Since the accident, Achebe has been confined to a motorized wheelchair and physical movement is difficult for him.

After he was discharged from the hospital, because of the trauma and physical difficulties associated with the accident, Achebe withdrew his agreement to go to Stanford. He needed a quiet place to reflect and to mend. At that time, Leon Botstein, the president of Bard College, approached him with an offer of an endowed chair: the Charles P. Stevenson Jr. Professorship of English. Botstein said:

> I went after Chinua Achebe because he is one of the great
> intellectual and ethical figures of our times. ...A great deal
> of muliticulturalism today is canned: It reduces and
> essentializes African and black experience. I thought it im-
> portant for students to hear an Achebe, who combines
> multiculturalism with wisdom.[9]

Achebe accepted the offer to move to Bard College, which is
located in Annandale-on-the Hudson in upstate New York.
Achebe chose Bard because it fitted with his need for a small,
quiet, intellectually stimulating environment that would enable him to recuperate and continue his intellectual activities.

It has not been easy for this world-class writer, whose inspiration has always been living and actively participating in
Nigeria's affairs. Bard built a wood-frame house, situated at
one end of a path, on the main entrance of the bucolic campus for his temporary home. Achebe's new home displays family photos, African sculptures, and beaded carvings, as well as
plaques from various universities honoring a great man.[10]

Achebe was unable to return to Nigeria, because his country was not only under the brutal and corrupt dictator, General Sani Abacha, but the fundamentals of civil order—including the availability of an adequate healthcare system—were
lacking.[11] Abacha came to power after the then ruling military
ruler, General Ibrahim Babangida refused to hand over power
to the democratically elected civilian, the colorful millionaire,
Chief Moshood Kashimawo Abiola. Babangida subsequently
annuled the June 12, 1993 elections and imposed his own puppet civilian government led by Ernest Shoneka, against the
Nigerian popular will. Abacha overthrew Shonekan's puppet
government, imprisoned Chief Abiola (who later died in
prison), and established the worst and most popularly despised
military rule in independent Nigeria's history. Abacha's reign

of terror eliminated many vocal Nigerians, including Ken Saro
Wiwa, the writer and environmental activist and champion of
the violated Ogoni rights in the Nigeria oil-producing Delta
region. Even the internationally eminent former Nigerian head
of state, General Olusegun Obasanjo, did not escape Abacha's
wrath. He was jailed, after being accused of plotting a coup.
Abacha's regime also charged Nobel Laureate Wole Soyinka
with treason. Of all of the regime's crimes, the government
execution of Ken Saro Wiwa—against all international outcry
and popular appeals for clemency—earned the most severe
international condemnation and showed the true nature of
Abacha's ruthless dictatorship. Abacha's rule wrecked havoc
on Nigeria's freedoms and infrastructure: he closed newspapers down, imprisoned or killed journalists and social activ-
ists, and stole and illegally transfered billions of public petro-
Nairas into private foreign accounts. Unexpectedly, on June
8, 1998, Abacha died of what the government officially designated as a heart attack.[12] Never in Nigeria's history has the
death of a leader been greeted with such national relief and
happiness. Abacha's successor, General Abdulsalam Abubakar,
returned the government to democratic civilian rule by orga-
nizing elections which were contested and won by General
Olusegun Obasanjo.

In August 1999, Achebe returned to Nigeria after nine years
of voluntary exile. His homecoming was greeted with excitement and celebration and dominated the headlines in leading
newspapers. The Saturday, August 28, 1999, issue of the
Lagos-based newspaper *This Day* showed his picture on the
front page with an article titled, "Homecoming of the Master
Storyteller." Even the president of Nigeria, General Olusegun
Obasanjo, hosted him at the state house with a homecoming
welcome. Asked about his long stay abroad for a writer whose
soul is Nigeria, Achebe said:

My nine years abroad have been bad, hopelessly bad. Things

have not been okay. I won't say I was completely surprised at the turn of events. But I didn't expect that we would hit the depth that we hit. It was almost a state of anarchy, the brutishness. But on reflection, once you begin the down-ward slope and you determine that nothing would stop you, you can't stop.[13]

Shuttling between hope and despair, when a fellow Nigerian optimistically mentioned, "Professor, we are happy that you are back, especially now that we are in democracy," Achebe was quick to correct him. "I would rather say, we are back on the path of democracy! Don't let us be deceived that we are in democracy, yet...."[14]

Ever the cautious thinker, Achebe appraised every response before he spoke. When asked about his thoughts on the pos-sibility of his compatriots rebuilding democracy and their civic fabric, Achebe humbly responded, "I am going to learn. All the things I know are what I have picked up in the media."[15] He then spoke about the need for civility in public discourse amongst Nigeria's peoples as that of a conversation befitting neighbors. He remarked, "The people of this country have been neighbors for so long. We have to cultivate the idea of talking things over...."[16] He had stern messages for the Babangida military government which annulled the elections which brought Abacha to power:

> I thought that something dangerous was happening... to over-throw the process of peaceful political transition. And that once that process was compromised, we [would] not hear the last of it. If you do not accept the result of a duly conducted election and you start a row over it, you will never settle the question of succession in the future.[17]

Achebe argued that even if some people did not believe that Chief Moshood Abiola was the right person to win the election, it was too late. Nigerians should have waited for him to serve his term and, at the end of the four years if not satisfied with his performance, then vote him out.[18]

As for the new Nigerian president, General Obasanjo, Achebe praised him for being the right person at this critical stage of Nigeria's history. Achebe argued,

> Obasanjo has experience— both military and civilian. He also has an experience which I consider more important; that is he was roughly handled by General Abacha so that if anybody is talking about tyranny and dictatorship, Obasanjo understands what they mean because he narrowly escaped death. That is a great qualification to run this new experiment.[19]

Nevertheless he remains unsure as to whether Obasanjo will succeed since so much depends on the cooperation and support of the Nigerian population.

Following his Nigeria trip, Achebe returned to Bard College with profound memories of home. Of his visit, he recalled, "I'm still very emotional about it. It's really a wonderful experience to connect again to people who share this culture, this land of Igbo and to be with people who have been treated badly by rulers."[20] Since his return, he had been busy with several speaking engagements across the United States, some to promote a new book of essays, *Home and Exile*. As he spoke, Achebe gestured with his hands sweeping the air in an arc. In an interview, remembering home, he said, "Nigeria is like a wobbly tripod, and its three major ethnic groups— the Hausa, Igbo and Yoruba, who frequently contest one another for power and turf are its unwieldy legs.... Nigeria refuses to stand on three legs."[21]

Perhaps, as one looks at Achebe's entire life, his immersion in Igbo culture, his education, and his ambivalence to Western culture, his complicated love for Nigeria, his pragmatism about Africa, what emerges is a concentric vision. That vision, although sometimes betrayed by the despair of present failures, nonetheless points to a stubborn hope. That hope comes only from someone who is a source of illumination, a teacher of light.

Chinua Achebe: Teacher of Light

After all is said and done,
After all the fanfare is gone,
We must remember Achebe, this wise soul,
Who gave us novels to fill our ricebowls.

We must remember his words,
This teacher who told us where rain shards
Began to beat us. This sage,
Who never lets ideas end in a wriggle,
Whether on stage or on page.

We must remember him
For telling us how Things Fell Apart;
Praise him to the brim
For a tragic tale told smart.
For Okonkwo is unbending Africa,
Heroic for defending the old order,
Lovable and rigid, shortsighted to his downfall.
Needed and needing, we deserve a better replica.
We need an open Africa, strong and sober.

We must remember him,
For our continent is No Longer at Ease.
We need redemptive Arrows of God; not arrogant
military teens.
To rescue our betrayed hopes from this trying
unease,
To avoid Anthills of the Savannah; to steer us into
better dreams.
To avoid the cult of the gun; to steer us into

Mightier streams.

We must remember him,
For we no longer need false Men of the People.
We need African patriots like him,
Whose rich thoughts and acts energize our people.

After all is said and done,
We must remember this Teacher
Did his job well, from dusk to dawn.
That he was simple in his art, clear, but no
preacher,
Yet the whole world learned from his wisdom.
Now, Earth, join us to celebrate his wisdom.
© *Tijan M. Sallah*[22]

NOTES

1. Ezenwa-Ohaeto, *Chinua Achebe*, pp. 275-278.
2. Emmanuel Obiechina, "In Praise of the Teacher: A Tribute to Chinua Achebe," unpublished, p. 2.
3. Ibid., p. 6.
4. Ezenwa-Ohaeto, *Chinua Achebe*, p. 277.
5. Winkler, "An African Writer," p. A9.
6. Jahman Anikulapo, "Nigeria on My Mind- Achebe," Lagos, Nigeria, *The Guardian*, vol. 16, no. 7,594, Saturday, August 28, 1999, p. 14.
7. Nduka Otiono, "Homecoming of the Master Storyteller," Lagos, Nigeria, *This Day*, vol. 5, no. 1588, August 28, 1999, p. 15.
8. Ezenwa-Ohaeto, *Chinua Achebe*, p. 278.
9. Winkler, "An African Writer," p. A12.
10. Gayle Feldman, "View of Home from Afar," *Publishers Weekly*, July 3, 2000, p. 40.
11. Somini Sengupta, "A Storyteller Far From Home: Healthcare, Not Politics, Prolongs a Nigerian Writer's Exile," *The New York Times*, The Arts, Monday, January 10, 2000, p.1.
12. CNN report "Nigerian Leader General Sani Abacha Dead" and "Abacha Known for Brutality,"June 8, 1998.
13. Anikulapo,"Nigeria on My Mind: Achebe," p. 14.
14. Ibid., p. 15.
15. Ibid.
16. Ibid.
17. Ibid.
18. Ibid.
19. Otiono, "Homecoming," p. 15.
20. Sengupta, "A Storyteller," p. 3.
21. Ibid.
22. A tribute poem by one of the co-authors of this book.

BIBLIOGRAPHY

Achebe, Chinua. *Things Fall Apart*, London: William Heinemann, 1958; New York: Anchor Books, Doubleday, 1994.

—————. *No Longer at Ease*, London: William Heinemann, 1960; New York: Anchor Books, Doubleday, 1994.

—————. *The Sacrificial Egg and Other Short Stories*, Onitsha, Nigeria: Etudo Ltd., 1962.

—————. *Arrow of God*, London: William Heinemann, 1964; New York: Anchor Books, Doubleday, 1989.

—————. *Chike and the River* (children's book), Cambridge: Cambridge University Press, 1966,.

—————. *A Man of the People*, London: William Heinemann, 1966; Anchor Books, Doubleday, 1989.

—————. *Beware Soul Brothers and Other Poems*. Enugu, Nigeria: Nwankwo-Ifejika, 1971; reprinted as *Christmas in Biafra and Other Poems*, Garden City, N.Y.: Anchor, Doubleday, 1973; reprinted as *Beware Soul Brother*. Oxford, England: Heinemann Educational Books, 1972.

—————. *Girls at War and Other Stories*. London: Heinemann Educational Books, 1972; Garden City, N.Y.: Anchor, Doubleday, 1973.

—————. (and John Iroaganachi). *How the Leopard Got His Claws* (children's book). Enugu, Nigeria: Nwamife, 1972; New York: The Third Press, 1973.

—————. *Morning Yet on Creation Day* (essays), London: Heinemann Educational Books, 1975; New York: Anchor, Doubleday, 1975.

—————. *The Drum* (children's book), Enugu: Fourth Dimension Publishers, 1977.

—————. *The Flute* (children's book), Enugu: Fourth Dimension Publishers, 1977.

—————. (Ed. with Obiora Udechukwu), *Aka Weta: Egwu Aguluagu, Egwu edeluede*, Nsukka: Okike Magazine, 1982.

—————. *The Trouble With Nigeria* (essays), Enugu: Fourth Dimension Publishers, 1983; London: Heinemann Educational Books, 1984.

—————. (Ed. with C.L. Innes), *African Short Stories*, London: Heinemann Educational Books, 1985.

—————. *Anthills of the Savannah*, London: William Heinemann, 1987; New York: Anchor Press, Doubleday, 1988.

—————. *The University and the Leadership Factor in Nigerian Politics* (pamphlet), Enugu: Abic Books and Equipment Ltd., 1988.

————. *Hopes and Impediments* (essays), London: Heinemann Educational Books, 1988; New York: Bantam Doubleday, 1989.

————. (Ed. with C.L. Innes), *Contemporary African Short Stories*, London: Heinemann Educational Books, 1990.

————. *Africa Is People* (a pamphlet), Washington, D.C.: The World Bank, Presidential Fellow Lecture Series, 1998, pp. 3-9.

————. *Home and Exile* (essays), Oxford: Oxford University Press, 2000.

————. "The role of the writer in a new nation," *Nigeria Magazine* 81, 1964, pp. 157-160.

————. "The Education of a 'British Protected' Child," *The Cambridge Review*, vol. 114, no. 2321, Cambridge, England,

————. "My Country and Me," *New African*, Life Section, No 11, London, England, June 1992, pp. 14-15.

————. "The Bane of Union: An appraisal of the consequences of Union Igbo for Igbo Language and Literature," *ANU Magazine*, 1, 1979, pp. 33-41.

————. "The Judge and I didn't go to Namibia," *Callaloo*, vol. 13, no. 1, Winter 1990, pp. 82-85.

Anikulapo, Jahman. "Nigeria on my mind— Chinua Achebe," *The Guardian*, Lagos, Saturday, August 28, 1999, pp. 14-16.

Awogbemila, Olu with Ndaeyo Uko, Amuzi Akpaka, Soji Omotunde and Sanya Ademiluyi. "The Master Craftsman: Tribute to a thinker and writer at 59," *This Week*, no. 152, November 27, 1989, pp. 14-17, 20,22-23.

Basden, G.T. *Among the Ibos of Nigeria*, London: Frank Cass & Co, 1966.

Berman, Edward H. "Christian Missions in Africa," in *African Reactions to Missionary Education*, edited by E.H. Berman, New York: Teachers College, Columbia University, 1975.

Brooks, Jerome. "Chinua Achebe: The Art of Fiction CXXXVIV," The *Paris Review*, vol. 35, no. 133, Winter 1994-1995, pp. 142-166.

Cary, Joyce. *Mister Johnson*, New York: New Directions Publishing Corporation, 1989.

Chinweizu, and Onwuchekwa Jemie and Ihechukwu Madubuike. *Toward the Decolonization of African Literature*, Washington, D.C.: Howard University Press, 1983.

Cox, Clinton. *Mark Twain: America's Humorist, Dreamer, Prophet*, New York: Scholastic Inc., 1998.

Emenyonu, Ernest. *The Rise of the Igbo Novel*, Ibadan: University Press Limited, 1978.

Friedman, Gayle. "Chinua Achebe: Views of Home From Afar," *Publishers Weekly*, July 3, 2000, pp. 40-41.

Innes, C. L. *Chinua Achebe*, Cambridge: Cambridge University Press, 1990.

Klein, Leonard S., ed. *African Literatures in the 20th Century*, New York: The Ungar Publishing Company, 1986.

Lindfors, Bernth, ed. *Conversations with Chinua Achebe*, Jackson: University Press of Mississippi, 1997.

————,ed. *Critical Perspectives on Chinua Achebe*, Washington, D.C.: Three Continents Press, 1978.

————. "Beating the White Man at His Own Game: Nigerian Reactions to the 1986 Nobel Prize in Literature," *Black American Literature Forum*, Wole Soyinka Issue, Part I, vol. 22, no. 3, Fall 1988, pp. 475-487.

Marshall, P.J., ed. *Cambridge Illustrated History of the British Empire*, Cambridge: Cambridge University Press, 1996.

Mazrui, Ali A. and Michael Tidy. *Nationalism and New States in Africa*, New Hampshire: Heinemann Educational Books, 1984.

Obasanjo, General Olusegun. *My Command: An Account of the Nigerian Civil War 1967-70*, London: Heinemann Educational Books, 1980.

Obiechina, Emmanuel. "In Praise of the Teacher: A Tribute to Chinua Achebe," Unpublished paper delivered at the 1990 conference, 'Eagle on Iroko: Chinua Achebe at 60', pp. 1-25.

Odogwu, Bernard. *No Place to Hide (Crisis and Conflicts Inside Biafra)*, Enugu: Fourth Dimension Publishing Co., Ltd., 1985.

Ogunbiyi, Yemi, ed. *Perspectives on Nigerian Literature: 1700 to The Present, Volume Two*, Lagos: Guardian Books Nigeria Ltd., 1988.

Ohaeto, Ezenwa. *Chinua Achebe: A biography*, Bloomington: Indiana University Press, 1997.

Ojiako, James Obioha. *13 Years of Military Rule 1966-79*, Lagos: Daily Times of Nigeria Ltd., 1979.

Okigbo, Christopher. *Labyrinth: Poems*, London: Heinemann Educational Books, 1971.

Omotunde, Soji. "Our Relationship is Profound," *This Week*, no. 152, November 27, 1989, p. 2.

Orwell, George. *A Collection of Essays*, Garden City, New York: Doubleday Anchor Books, 1954.

Otiono, Nduka. "Homecoming of the Master Storyteller," *This Day*, The Saturday Newspaper, vol. 5, no. 1588, August 28, 1999, pp. 14-16.

Petersen, Kirsten Holst and Anna Rutherford, eds. *Chinua Achebe: A Celebration*, Oxford: Heinemann Educational Books, 1990.

Robinson, Ronald, John Gallagher and Alice Denny. *Africa and the Victorians: The Climax of Imperialism*, Garden City, New York: Anchor Books, 1968.

Sallah, Tijan M and Nkozi Okonjo-Iweala. " Personal Interview with Chinua Achebe," March 1995, Unpublished.

Sengupta, Somini. "A Storyteller Far From Home: Health Care, Not Politics, Prolongs a Nigerian Writer's Exile," *The New York Times*, Monday, January 10, 2000, pp. 2-3.

Soyinka, Wole. *The Man Died*, Ibadan: Spectrum Books Limited, 1990.

Swedish Academy. "Press Release (October 1986): The Nobel Prize in Literature 1986— Wole Soyinka," reproduced in *Black American Literature Forum*, Wole Soyinka Issue, Part 1, vol. 22, no. 3, Fall 1988, pp. 425-426.

Tidy, Michael with Donald Leeming. *A History of Africa: 1840-1914*, New York: Africana Publishing Company, 1981.

Trueheart,Charles. "Chinua Achebe & the Politics of Art: The Novelist's Tales From A World Turned Upside Down," *The Washington Post*, Tuesday, February 16, 1988, pp. D3, D4.

Tsuruta, Dorothy Randall. "James Baldwin and Chinua Achebe in Dialogue to Define Aesthetics," *The Black Scholar*, vol. 12, no. 2, March/April 1981, pp. 72-79.

Twain, Mark. *King Leopold's Soliloquy*, New York: International Publishers, 1970.

Uchendu, Victor C. *The Igbo of Southeast Nigeria*, New York: Harcourt Brace Jovanovich College Publishers, 1965.

Winkler, Karen J. "An African Writer at a Crossroads: Now at Bard College, Chinua Achebe has become an influential figure in Western literary circles," *The Chronicle of Higher Education*, January 12, 1994, pp. A9, A12.

Wren, Robert M. *Achebe's World: The Historical and Cultural Context of the Novels*, Washington, D.C., Three Continents Press, 1980.

———. *Those Magical Years: The Making of Nigerian Literature At Ibadan: 1948-1966*, Washington, D.C.: Three Continents Press, 1991.

INDEX